REGIONAL ITALIAN COOKING

Ruth Bauder Kershner

WEATHERVANE BOOKS
New York

contents

introduction

When we think of Italian cuisine, we often think only of pasta, pizza, veal Parmesan, and minestrone. We fail to realize the variety and diversity of Italy and her cuisine. The Italians are an independent people with an appreciation of fine art, great wine, beautiful music, and good food. Family life centered around the dinner table. Regional specialties were guarded like precious jewels with great pride and jealousy and not shared with neighboring city-states.

The Italian peninsula encompasses over 116,000 square miles and 19 separate provinces and regions. The climate varies from the cold, severe Alpine winters of the north to the warm, sunny Mediterranean south. Italy is blessed with over 2500 miles of coastline. The Appenine Mountains stretch down the peninsula like a backbone dividing the area in two. There are many beautiful lakes and a wealth of rivers dotting the peninsula. Many towns grew in relative isolation. Over the centuries, individual city-states grew, prospered and vied with each other for power. Italy was finally united under one monarchy only a little over 100 years ago.

Historically, Italy has been heavily influenced by her neighbors, especially Austria, Switzerland, France, Germany, the Baltics and even the Arabs. Remnants of invasions and occupations remain in the cuisine today. In the south of Italy, the fine art of making ice cream and fruit ices was introduced by the Arabs. In the Alto-Adige, Austrian influence is seen in the strudel, schnitzel, and sauerkraut that are served. Remnants of the ancient history of the peninsula are still retained. Polenta stems from Roman times when a thick porridge-like mixture called "polmentum" was served. Out of all these influences comes a rich and varied cuisine, at once as old as ancient Rome and as new as a shiny Ferrari, rich with regional specialties and history. For this book, only 5 distinctive regions were selected to introduce you to the world of Italian regional cuisine. Each region will be briefly discussed here to introduce you to its unique characteristics.

I. Milan (Lombardy)

Milan is the large metropolitan commercial center dominating Lombardy, a large northern province. The world famous opera house, La Scala, is located in Milan and it is considered to be a very cosmopolitan city. Milanese cooking is hearty as befits the colder northern Italian climate. Polenta and rice from the Po valley are substituted for the pasta served in southern Italy. Butter rather than oil is used in cooking and the region is famous for fine cheese. A wide variety of vegetables and fruits (especially grapes) are grown in this region. Long, slow cooking has always been a hallmark of Milanese cookery. Delicious soups and stews simmer all day on the back of the stove. Beef, chicken, pork and veal are favored in this area. Tomatoes are used only sparingly in cooking in this area and sage is the predominate herb.

Many Milanese dishes are world-famous. A soup based on chicken broth with garlic toast and a poached egg in it, is said to have originated in Pavia in honor of a visit by King Francis I of France. Osso Bucco and Risotto Alla Milanese are found frequently on European menus. Torrone, a nougat candy, and panettone are Christmas favorites and are shipped all over Italy. Campari, a bitter Italian aperitif is also made in this region.

II. Florence (Tuscany)

Tuscany is called the "heartland" of Italy. The people here are robust and direct. The Tuscan dialect, which is considered to be one of the purest forms of the Italian language, is still used. Cooking relies on simple ingredients of the best quality. Florence, the city of the Medicis, overshadows all with her brilliance. Beef, beans, and Chianti are characteristic of the region. Some of the finest cattle in Italy are produced in the Chiana Valley. Chianina cattle grow rapidly to a very large weight, making for very tender eating. Beans are cooked in enumerable ways and can be included in every course except dessert. True Chianti Classico comes from the grapes grown in the region between Florence and Sienna and is sold in straw-covered bottles. Olive oil is the principal cooking fat of Tuscany, and Lucca produces some of the finest oil in Italy. Zuppa di fagioli, bistecca alla fiorentina and Chianti would make an excellent Florentine meal.

III. Venice (Veneto)

During the Middle Ages, Venice was the European capital of the spice trade supplying coffee, sugar, salt, pepper, and spices to not only her own country but also much of the European continent. Today, the Doges' Palaces remain along the numerous canals winding through Venice. Venice and all Veneto still depend heavily on the sea for food and income. Seafood in many forms is featured throughout the region. Scampi and risi-bisi are a favorite Venetian combination. Rice prepared in many ways, as well as polenta, are the starchy staples of the diet. The area around Vincenza is renowned for its turkeys, a gift from the New World much enjoyed by the Italians.

Veneto produces many fine wines well worth looking for to accompany fine Italian food. Valpolicella and Bardolino are both red wines from the region around Verona. Soave, a mild delicate white wine, is considered one of the best Italian wines.

IV. Rome (Latium)

In Rome the cooking of both the north and south of Italy meet. Whole lamb, kid, or suckling pig may be roasted for special occasions. The flat noodles of Northern Italy, as well as the spaghetti and macaroni of the South, are served. Bacon, lard, and olive oil may be used as the basis for cooking. The rich, volcanic soil around Rome produces superior vegetables. Celery, broccoli, artichokes, peas, and lettuce are special favorites. Delicious soups, featuring vegetables are an important part of the daily fare. Sauces based on tomatoes come into more frequent use in the area surrounding Rome. The warmer climate provides the 120 sunny days necessary for good tomato culture. Roman cuisine combines these delicious elements to make cannelloni and suppli. Granita and gelati are the favorite Roman desserts of which they are very proud. In addition many fine wines come from the area surrounding Rome. The most well known are Orvieto, Frascati, and Est! Est! Est!

V. Naples (Campania)

Naples is a bustling port filled with life. You can eat at any hour of the day or night. Small pizzas, panzarotti, and even oysters and other seafood are available from street vendors. Life is crowded, noisy and busy. Mount Vesuvius dominates the landscape and the ruins of Pompei and Herculaneum are nearby. Campania is more fortunate than other parts of Southern Italy, for Vesuvius has provided some rich volcanic soil. Large quantities of fresh vegetables are grown and figure prominently in Neopolitan cooking. Eggplant, tomatoes and peppers are special favorites.

Pasta is the backbone of the diet. Since macaroni and spaghetti are made with hard wheat flour, they are extremely difficult to knead. Most Neopolitans prefer to purchase ready-made factory pasta and then prepare delicious homemade sauces. Seafood also figures prominently in the Neopolitan diet, forming the basis of soups, stews, sauces for pasta, or simply dipped in batter and fried. Olive oil is the fat used most often in this type of cooking.

Pizza is said to have originated in Naples and a fine art is made of its preparation. Fresh bread dough is rolled, topped with a fresh tomato pommerola for which Naples is famous, topped with meat or fish, and then with grated cheeses. The result is a very satisfying culinary creation.

Meat is used sparingly in Neopolitan cooking. Grazing land is at a minimum and meat is not wasted. In addition to the use of oregano and sweet basil, rosemary, thyme, and mint show the Arabic influence in the South of Italy. Sweets are generally reserved for holidays, weddings, and christenings and may then be quite elaborate in character. The wines of Campania are generally drunk within the region and not exported. The best wines are those without vintage which make their way to the everyday table.

Finally, a few words should be said about the Italian way of eating, since it differs from our own. Upon waking in the morning, a light breakfast consisting of coffee or coffee mixed with milk and bread or a roll is usually eaten. The main meal of the day is eaten leisurely (especially on holidays) around 1 P.M. and is very family oriented. Antipasto is served first, with wine or aperitifs, such as Campari. The antipasto may be as simple as fresh celery served with salt and pepper and olive oil or it may be quite complicated involving several sliced meats and cheese. Next comes minestrone (soup) or pasta asciutta (rice, noodle or spaghetti dish). This will be followed by a meat dish with accompanying vegetables or salad. Then fruit and cheese or perhaps pastry are served for dessert. Coffee is served as a separate course at the end of the meal. Bread and wine or mineral water always accompany the meal. The coffee bars are open in the late afternoon serving coffee as well as apperitifs. Supper is eaten late and is relatively a light meal.

Above all, food represents hospitality for the Italian and visitors are always welcomed. Regional

Italian cooking has many delicious surprises to offer. Experiment with the recipes in this book and you will surely enjoy some delicious, new experiences!

guide to unusual ingredients:

Most of the ingredients necessary for fine Italian cooking are available at your local grocery store. The Italian kitchen is a seasonal kitchen. The Italian cook selects only ingredients of the highest quality that are fresh and at their peak of flavor. You may find a trip to a local Italian grocer or delicatessen worthwhile for meats, cheeses, and imported items for experimentation. The following notes may help you in the selection of ingredients:

Oil: Olive oil is a basic ingredient in most southern Italian recipes. Select a good quality imported or domestic olive oil, as it adds a subtle flavor. If you must, substitute any mild-flavored vegetable oil, for example soy, cottonseed, or safflower oil.

Cheese: Cheese is a staple of the Italian diet. Summarized here are a few of the basic cheeses used in cooking.

    Ricotta: This is a fresh cheese that is soft and creamy in texture and mild in flavor. It may be made from whole or partly-skimmed milk. If you can not find ricotta cheese try substituting pot or farmer cheese.

    Mozzarella: This is a bland white cheese that melts easily. It is readily available in most supermarkets. Jack or Meunster cheese might be substituted if Mozzarella is unavailable.

    Parmesan Cheese: This is a hard grating cheese. If you possibly can, buy a wedge of well-aged cheese and grate it yourself when you are ready to use it. Grated Parmesan cheese purchased in cans lacks flavor and body. Try freshly-grated Parmesan and you will never forget the difference.

Prosciutto: Prosciutto is cured Italian ham. If unavailable substitute Smithfield, country ham, or pepper ham. Boiled ham will give very little flavor.

Italian-style plum tomatoes: Italian plum tomatoes are available in most supermarkets. They are stronger in flavor and slightly more acid in taste. On the vine they are small, very red, firm, and plum-shaped rather than globular. Italian plum tomatoes may be domestic or imported.

Pasta: Pasta is the collective name applied to more than 500 varieties of spaghetti, noodles, macaroni, and like products, made from flour, water, and sometimes eggs. The two basic classes of pasta are flat noodles and tubular macaronis. Flat noodles are more commonly seen in the north of Italy and may be made at home. The tubular macaronis seen in the south of Italy are generally purchased ready-made as the dough is very stiff and hard to handle. Imported or domestic pasta may be used depending on your preference. In a simple recipe calling for cooked pasta topped with sauce, the various macaronis may be used interchangeably. Be sure to read the directions carefully on the package and cook in plenty of boiling salted water until "al dente". This terms means literally "to the tooth." The pasta should resist a little when you bite into it. It should never be mushy. Drain quickly and serve immediately. The pasta waits for no man.

Herbs and spices: Herbs and spices are widely used in Italian cookery. A well-stocked spice shelf will generally meet all of your needs. Among the more frequently used herbs and spices are: oregano, sweet basil, sage, rosemary, thyme, and garlic. Of course, the fresher the herbs the better. In Italy, they are picked fresh from the garden. You may not be familiar with saffron. This spice comes from the dried stamens of the crocus. It was highly prized in the Middle Ages for its deep orange color. It is expensive and available in very small quantities in the gourmet section of the grocery or department store. If it is unavailable, omit it from the recipe.

Milan (Lombardy)

figs and prosciutto
fichi e prosciutto

4 fresh ripe figs
½ pound prosciutto

Chill figs thoroughly; peel. Cut pointed tips from figs; peel in sections by sliding knife under skins. Cut figs into quarters.

Arrange on small platter alternately with rolled prosciutto slices. Makes 4 servings.

soup with meatballs
zuppa di frittelle

2 (10¾ ounce) cans
  condensed beef broth
2 soup cans water
2 tablespoons tomato paste
1 teaspoon crumbled sweet
  basil

meatballs
½ pound lean ground beef
¼ pound ground pork or
  milk sausage
¼ cup fine dry bread
  crumbs
1 egg, lightly beaten
¼ cup finely chopped onion
Salt and pepper

¼ cup raw long-grain rice
2 cups washed, coarsely
  shredded fresh spinach
  leaves

Combine beef broth and water in large saucepan; bring to boil. Dissolve tomato paste in broth; add basil. Cover; keep hot.

In mixing bowl combine meats, bread crumbs, egg, onion, and seasonings; mix well. Form into meatballs; use 1 scant tablespoon meat mixture for each.

Drop meatballs 1 by 1 into boiling broth. Cover; cook 10 minutes. Add rice; stir gently. Cover; cook 20 minutes. Add spinach; cook 5 minutes.

Garnish with chopped parsley, if desired. Serve with crusty bread. Makes 4 servings.

Note: Swiss chard can be substituted for spinach if desired.

pavian soup
zuppa pavese

3 tablespoons olive oil
1 clove garlic, peeled
4 slices crusty Italian bread, 1½ inches thick
2 (13-ounce) cans regular-strength chicken broth (4 cups homemade
  chicken stock can be substituted)
4 eggs
4 tablespoons freshly grated Parmesan cheese

Heat oil in small, heavy skillet. Add garlic clove; sauté until browned. Discard garlic. Add bread slices to skillet; sauté until golden, turning once. Remove from pan; drain on paper towels.

Heat chicken broth to boiling in medium saucepan.

Break eggs into bowl or saucer; slide 1 by 1 into hot broth. Poach eggs over low heat until white is set. Remove with slotted spoon; keep warm. Strain broth; heat to boiling.

Place 1 slice toasted bread in each soup plate. Top each bread slice with poached egg. Pour hot broth over egg and toast. Sprinkle each bowl with 1 tablespoon Parmesan. Serve immediately. Makes 4 servings.

butterball soup
gnocchi al brodo

1½ tablespoons butter
1 egg yolk
3 tablespoons flour
1 tablespoon grated
  Parmesan cheese
⅛ teaspoon salt
White pepper
Dash of nutmeg
1 egg white, stiffly beaten
4½ cups clear beef broth

Thoroughly cream butter and egg yolk in small bowl. Add flour, cheese, and seasonings; mix well. Fold in egg white.

Bring broth to boil in large saucepan. Reduce heat to moderate; drop dough by teaspoons into boiling broth. Cover pan; simmer 10 minutes.

Ladle into soup bowls. Garnish if desired with chopped parsley, or add cooked julienne-cut carrots and celery. Makes 4 servings.

little dumplings
gnocchi

These can be served as a pasta course or an accompaniment to a meat dish.

4 medium potatoes
1½ to 1¾ cups all-purpose flour
1 teaspoon salt
¼ teaspoon white pepper

Wash, peel, and dice potatoes. (You should have approximately 3½ cups diced potatoes.) Cook potatoes in boiling salted water until tender. Drain well. Mash potatoes; immediately add enough flour to make thick dough. Add salt and pepper. Divide dough into 4 equal parts. Using ¼ of dough, on floured surface roll into cylinder ½ inch in diameter. Cut into pieces ½ inch long.

Flour tines of fork; slightly flatten each gnocchi. Place on lightly floured towel until ready to cook. Handle remaining dough in same manner; add more flour if dough becomes sticky.

Cook gnocchi in large kettle of gently boiling salted water. Drop gnocchi into kettle 1 by 1 until bottom of pot is covered; cook approximately 5 minutes, until they float to surface. Remove with slotted spoon; drain well. Serve immediately topped with marinara or meat sauce. Makes 4 servings.

baked gnocchi
gnocchi al forno

1 recipe cooked gnocchi
¼ cup butter or margarine
¼ cup grated Parmesan cheese

Place gnocchi in casserole.

Lightly brown butter in small, heavy skillet over moderate heat. Pour butter over gnocchi; sprinkle with cheese. Bake at 375°F 10 minutes; broil until lightly browned.

Note: Gnocchi can be prepared and frozen in single layer on cookie sheet before cooking. Store in plastic bag.

Boil as usual before serving. Cooking time will be slightly increased.

marinated vegetable salad
insalata vegetali marinata

2 quarts water
2 teaspoons salt
1 (10-ounce) package Romano beans, partially defrosted
1 (10-ounce) package cauliflower
2 carrots, peeled, thinly sliced
1 medium zucchini, sliced ¼ inch thick
2 cloves garlic
1 teaspoon salt
¼ cup white wine vinegar
6 tablespoons olive oil
¼ teaspoon pepper
½ cup sliced ripe olives
1 medium onion, peeled, sliced, separated into rings

Combine water and salt in Dutch oven; bring to boil. Add beans, cauliflower, and carrots. Cook 4 minutes. Add zucchini; cook 3 minutes. Drain in colander.

Peel garlic cloves; place on wooden board. Sprinkle with salt; mash well with side of knife. Combine garlic, vinegar, oil, and pepper in bottom of salad bowl; mix well. Add vegetables, olives, and onion; mix gently. Cover; refrigerate several hours or overnight before serving. Makes 6 servings.

macaroni salad with salami
insalata di pasta e salami

1 cup cooked tubetti or other short macaroni
½ cup chopped green pepper
¼ cup chopped celery
½ cup cooked frozen peas, drained (undercook slightly so they retain their shape)
½ cup salami strips
2 sweet pickles, finely chopped

salad dressing
½ cup mayonnaise or salad dressing
3 tablespoons milk
1 tablespoon lemon juice
Salt, pepper, and cayenne

garnish
2 hard-cooked eggs, peeled, quartered
2 medium tomatoes, peeled, quartered
2 tablespoons chopped parsley

In mixing bowl lightly combine tubetti, pepper, celery, peas, salami, and pickles.

Combine mayonnaise, milk, and lemon juice in a small bowl. Season to taste with salt, pepper, and cayenne. Pour over salad; mix gently. Place in serving bowl; chill well.

Garnish with eggs and tomatoes; sprinkle with parsley. Makes 4 servings.

butterball soup

macaroni salad with salami

veal chops milanese

veal chops milanese
costolette di vitello milanese

4 veal sirloin chops, about 6 ounces each (1½ pounds total)
⅓ cup flour
Salt and pepper
2 eggs, beaten
⅔ cup dry bread crumbs
⅓ cup grated Parmesan cheese
¼ cup olive oil
2 tablespoons butter

Wipe veal with damp cloth.

Combine flour, salt, and pepper on piece of waxed paper. Dredge chops in flour mixture; shake off excess. Dip in beaten eggs, then in mixture of bread crumbs and cheese, coating well.

Combine oil and butter in large heavy skillet; heat until foam subsides. Add chops; cook over moderate heat, turning occasionally, until golden brown. Drain on paper towels. Serve immediately.

Garnish with lemon slices; serve with browned butter or tomato sauce if desired. Makes 4 servings.

veal shanks milanese
osso bucco

3 pounds veal shank, sawed into thick slices with marrow intact
Salt and pepper
Flour
6 tablespoons butter
1 medium onion, peeled, chopped
1 clove garlic, peeled, minced
2 carrots, peeled, diced
2 stalks celery, chopped
½ cup white wine
¼ cup chicken broth
1 bay leaf
¼ teaspoon thyme

gremolata
2 tablespoons finely chopped parsley
1 clove garlic, peeled, finely minced
1 teaspoon finely grated lemon peel

Wipe veal with damp cloth. Season with salt and pepper. Dredge in flour; shake off excess.

Heat butter in deep skillet or Dutch oven. Add veal; brown well on all sides. Remove from pan. Add onion and garlic; sauté until tender. Add vegetables wine, chicken broth, and seasonings. Add veal shanks, standing on their sides to prevent marrow falling from bone during cooking. Bring mixture to boil. Cover pan tightly; reduce heat to simmer. Cook approximately 1 hour, until veal is tender. If mixture looks dry at any time, add a little broth.

Meanwhile, combine gremolata ingredients; mix well.

Transfer veal to heated platter. Pour sauce over meat; sprinkle with gremolata.

Serve with rissotto or plain cooked pasta. Makes 4 servings.

sausage with lentils
zampone con lenticchie in umido

This dish is traditionally served in Italy on New Year's Day and is said to bring good luck!

2 cups dried lentils
8 cups water
1 ounce salt pork, diced
2 large tomatoes, peeled, diced
1 garlic clove; peeled
1 bay leaf
2 teaspoons salt
Freshly ground pepper
1 cotechino sausage or
1 zampone (about 2 pounds)

Wash lentils; pick over well to remove foreign matter. Place lentils in large saucepan. Add water, salt pork, tomatoes, garlic, bay leaf, salt, and pepper. Bring to boil over moderate heat. Skim foam from surface of cooking liquid. Reduce heat to low; simmer uncovered, stirring occasionally until lentils are soft and liquid almost evaporated. (Cooking time should be 45 minutes to 1 hour.) If liquid evaporates too quickly, add a little water.

Meanwhile, prick sausage well. Place in large pot; add water to cover. Bring to boil. Reduce heat to low; simmer 1 hour, until tender. Remove from pan; cool slightly. Slice; place on platter. Remove bay leaf and garlic clove from lentils. Spoon lentils around sausage; serve. Makes 6 servings.

Note: Cotechino and zampone are usually available in Italian delicatessens around the New Year. If unavailable, substitute 1½ pounds Italian sausage. Prick well; cook in ½ inch water until water evaporates; brown in own fat.

mixed vegetables milanese-style

vegetali misti alla milanese

3 slices bacon, diced
1 medium onion, peeled, sliced
1 red pepper, cleaned and cut into strips
3 carrots, peeled, sliced
2 medium potatoes, peeled, diced
½ cup chicken broth
1 (10-ounce) package frozen tiny peas
Salt and pepper

Cook bacon in large saucepan until crisp. Remove with slotted spoon; reserve. Add onion; sauté 2 minutes. Add pepper, carrots, potatoes, and chicken broth; bring to boil. Reduce heat to low; cook, covered, 15 minutes, until vegetables are crisp-tender. Add peas; simmer 5 minutes. Season with salt and pepper. Sprinkle with bacon; serve. Makes 4 to 5 servings.

mixed vegetables milanese-style

pasta with cream sauce
agnolotti con crema

pasta dough
2 cups all-purpose flour
1 teaspoon salt
3 eggs
2 teaspoons olive oil
1 tablespoon water

filling
2 tablespoons olive oil
¼ cup finely chopped onion
¼ pound ground veal
1 egg
1 cup cooked finely chopped chicken breast
⅛ pound finely chopped prosciutto
¼ teaspoon crushed rosemary
⅛ teaspoon nutmeg
Salt and pepper

cream sauce
3 tablespoons butter
6 tablespoons flour
Salt and pepper
1½ cups chicken broth
1½ cups light cream
½ cup freshly grated Parmesan cheese
⅛ teaspoon ground nutmeg

Prepare pasta dough. Combine flour and salt in mixing bowl. Combine eggs, oil, and water; mix well. Add to flour; mix to form stiff dough. Turn out onto board; knead 5 minutes. Cover with plastic wrap; let rest 30 minutes.

While dough rests, prepare filling. Heat oil in small, heavy skillet. Add onion; sauté until tender. Add veal; cook, stirring, until meat is crumbly and lightly browned. Transfer mixture to mixing bowl; cool slightly. Add remaining filling ingredients; mix well.

Divide pasta dough into 4 parts. Cover any dough not being used, to prevent drying. Roll dough, one part at a time, on lightly floured surface to 1/16 inch thick. Cut into 3-inch circles with round cutter or glass. Reroll scraps. Place heaping ½ teaspoon filling on each round. Dampen edge of circle with a little water. Fold into half-moon shape; seal. With folded edge toward you, bring two ends together; pinch. (Finished pasta looks like small circular hats with cuffs.) Place pasta on tray; cover with towel until ready to cook, or freeze for future use.

Prepare sauce. Melt butter in medium saucepan. Add flour, salt, and pepper; mix well. Cook 1 minute. Gradually stir in broth. Cook, stirring constantly, until thickened. Remove from heat; stir in cream. Return to heat; cook, stirring constantly, until thickened. Add cheese and nutmeg. Keep sauce warm while cooking pasta.

Cook pasta 10 minutes in large amount boiling salted water, with small amount oil added. Drain well. Serve immediately, topped with cream sauce.

Sprinkle with additional Parmesan cheese, if desired. Agnolotti can also be served with marinara sauce. Makes 6 servings or about 80 agnolotti.

Note: If available, use pasta machine for rolling dough.

rice pilaf
risotto

4 tablespoons butter
1 cup medium-grain or short-grain rice (preferably Italian)
4 tablespoons finely minced onion
2 tablespoons dry white wine
Pinch of saffron
4 cups hot chicken broth
2 tablespoons grated Parmesan cheese

Melt 3 tablespoons butter in heavy saucepan. Add rice and onion; sauté until lightly browned, stirring constantly. Add wine; cook until absorbed.

Dissolve saffron in chicken broth. Add broth to rice little at a time; continue cooking, stirring constantly, until all liquid is absorbed and rice is tender and creamy in consistency. (This should take 18 to 20 minutes.) Add remaining butter and cheese; mix well. Let cheese melt; serve immediately. Makes 4 servings.

soft italian nougat
torrone

1 cup honey
2⅓ cups whole hazelnuts
2 cups whole blanched almonds
1 cup sugar
2 tablespoons water
2 egg whites
2 teaspoons vanilla extract

Thoroughly grease cookie sheet with no sides; reserve.

Place honey in top of double boiler over boiling water; cook, stirring occasionally, 1 hour or to hard-ball stage (255°F) on candy thermometer.

Meanwhile place hazelnuts on cookie sheet; toast at 375°F 15 minutes. Place on tea towel; rub off skins; reserve.

Place almonds on cookie sheet; toast 10 minutes; set aside.

Combine sugar and water in heavy pan; cook, stirring occasionally, until caramelized. Keep warm.

Beat egg whites until stiff but not dry. When honey has reached desired temperature, beat egg whites into honey, tablespoon at a time with wooden spoon while continuing to cook. Mixture will become white and fluffy. Beat in caramelized sugar, then vanilla. Fold in nuts. Spread on prepared cookie sheet in rectangle 1½ inches thick. Cool completely; cut into 1 × 2-inch pieces. Wrap in waxed paper or cellophane. Makes about 32 (1 × 2-inch) pieces.

holiday fruit bread
panettone

½ cup milk, scalded, cooled to lukewarm
½ cup sugar
¼ cup soft butter or margarine
¾ teaspoon salt
2 packages active dry yeast
½ cup lukewarm water (105 to 115°F)
2 eggs, beaten
4¾ to 5½ cups sifted all-purpose flour
½ cup diced candied citron
½ cup dark or golden raisins
½ cup chopped walnuts
¾ teaspoon anise extract
3 tablespoons melted butter

Combine milk, sugar, ¼ cup butter, and salt in large mixing bowl.

Dissolve yeast in water. Add yeast mixture, eggs, and 1 cup flour to milk mixture. Beat with electric mixer 2 minutes on medium speed. Add 2 cups flour; mix well. Cover; let rise in warm place, free of drafts, until double in bulk (1½ to 2 hours).

Stir down batter.

Combine citron, raisins, and nuts. Alternately add fruit mixture and remaining flour, stirring well, to make soft dough. Stir in anise extract. Turn out onto lightly floured board; knead until smooth and elastic. Place in greased bowl. Cover; let rise in warm place until double in bulk (45 minutes to 1 hour).

Meanwhile, grease 2 (7-inch) cake pans. Attach a 2-inch greased brown-paper collar to pans. Greased coffee cans can also be used or bread can be shaped into round loaves and placed on cookie sheet. Punch dough down; divide into 2 balls. Place in prepared pans far apart on greased cookie sheet. Cover; let rise until double in bulk. Brush with melted butter; bake 20 to 25 minutes, until loaves sound hollow when tapped.

Remove from pan; cool on rack. Serve plain or toasted on Christmas morning with butter. Makes 2 loaves.

Florence (Tuscany)

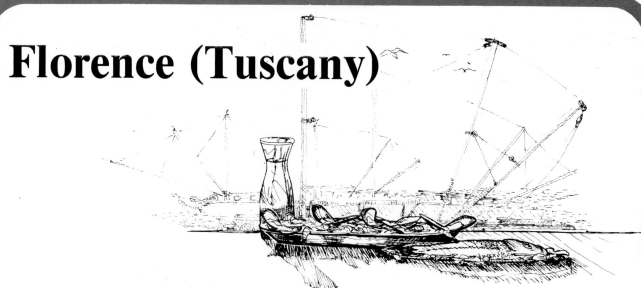

liver pâté on toasted bread rounds
crostini

½ pound chicken livers
3 tablespoons butter
1 small onion, chopped
1 clove garlic, minced
2 tablespoons white wine
½ teaspoon crumbled sage
Salt and pepper
2 teaspoons minced capers
1 teaspoon anchovy paste
Rounds of Italian bread, sliced ½ inch thick

Trim livers; remove all membrane and fat. Rinse under cold water; pat dry on paper towels.

Melt butter in small, heavy skillet. Add livers, onion, and garlic; sauté until livers are lightly browned. Add wine and seasonings. Cover; simmer 10 minutes. Put mixture through food mill. Return to skillet. Add capers and anchovy paste; mix well. Simmer 5 minutes.

Toast bread slices in oven until crisp and golden; spread thickly with liver pâté. Makes 4 servings.

Note: Bread can also be toasted in hot garlic-flavored olive oil. This makes a richer, more highly seasoned appetizer.

spinach dumplings

spinach dumplings
gnocchi verdi

1 (10-ounce) package frozen spinach, thawed
1 pound ricotta cheese
1 egg
½ cup grated Parmesan cheese
½ teaspoon salt
¼ teaspoon pepper
¼ teaspoon freshly grated nutmeg
½ cup all-purpose flour
¼ cup flour for coating gnocchi
Melted butter
Freshly grated Parmesan cheese for topping

Place spinach in sieve; press with back of spoon until dry. In mixing bowl combine ricotta, spinach, and egg; mix well. Stir in Parmesan and seasonings. Add all-purpose flour; mix well.

Place ¼ cup flour on plate. Form rounded teaspoons of spinach-and-cheese mixture into dumplings by coating lightly with flour and rolling between palms of hands to form round balls. Place on waxed paper in single layer until ready to cook.

Bring 4 quarts salted water to boil in large kettle. Drop gnocchi 1 by 1 into boiling water until bottom of pot is filled with gnocchi in single layer. When gnocchi are done, they will rise to surface of water. Remove with slotted spoon; drain well. Place in warm serving bowl. Continue until all gnocchi are cooked.

Drizzle with melted butter, sprinkle with Parmesan cheese; serve. Makes 6 servings.

19

beef stew

beef stew
manzo in umido

Many Northern Italian dishes begin with what is called "battuto," which means to chop together. In the American kitchen, if a recipe calls for onion and garlic, we chop each ingredient separately and add it to the skillet. In Italy, a number of vegetables and salt pork or bacon are chopped together so that each takes flavor from the other. This method is used here to make a delicious beef stew.

2 ounces salt pork	
1 medium onion	**1½ pounds lean beef cubes**
1 clove garlic, peeled	**1 cup red wine (preferably Chianti)**
1 medium carrot	**½ cup tomato sauce**
1 celery stalk with leaves	**1 bay leaf**
2 sprigs parsley	**1 teaspoon crumbled oregano**
2 tablespoons oil	**Salt and pepper**

Roughly chop pork, onion, garlic, carrot, celery, and parsley; combine. Mince together on wooden board until all ingredients are very finely chopped. Place *battuto* in Dutch oven or large heavy frypan. Add oil; sauté until pork is lightly browned and vegetables limp.

Wipe beef cubes with damp cloth; add to pan. Brown on all sides. Drain off excess fat. Add wine, tomato sauce, and seasonings; bring to boil. Reduce heat to low; cook 2 hours, until meat is very tender.

Garnish with chopped parsley if desired. Makes 4 servings.

20

pork roast florentine-style
arrosto di maiale alla fiorentina

1 (4-pound) pork loin roast
2 tablespoons olive oil
3 cloves garlic, peeled, cut into thirds
1 teaspoon crumbled dried rosemary
Fresh-ground black pepper

Wipe pork with damp cloth. Rub with oil. Cut 9 slits in fat on top; insert 1 garlic sliver in each slit. Rub with rosemary; grind pepper over roast. Place fat-side-up on rack in shallow roasting pan. Roast at 325°F approximately 2 hours or until meat thermometer registers, 175°F. Remove from oven; let rest 15 minutes before carving.

Small peeled potatoes and small whole white onions can be added to roasting pan last hour of cooking. Turn vegetables several times during cooking. Makes 4 to 6 servings.

breast of chicken with italian ham
petti di pollo con prosciutto

4 individual chicken breasts, (about ½ pound each), skinned, boned
Salt and pepper
1 teaspoon crumbled dried leaf sage
¼ pound prosciutto, thinly sliced
4 tablespoons butter
1 small onion, minced
1 clove garlic, minced
½ pound mushrooms, cleaned, sliced
¼ cup chicken broth
¼ cup white wine
2 tablespoons chopped fresh parsley

Place chicken between sheets of waxed paper; pound with flat side of cleaver or bottom of heavy bottle to form cutlets of even thickness. Remove waxed paper. Season with salt and pepper; sprinkle with sage. Evenly distribute ham atop chicken. Fold in half; secure with toothpick.

Melt butter in heavy skillet. Add chicken; cook over moderate heat, turning until lightly browned. Remove from pan.

Add onion and garlic to pan; cook 1 minute. Add mushrooms; cook until mushroom liquid evaporates. Return chicken to skillet; spoon mushrooms over them. Add chicken broth and wine. Cover; simmer 20 minutes.

Transfer to platter; cover chicken with mushrooms. Pour over pan juices; sprinkle with parsley; serve. Makes 4 servings.

breast of chicken with italian ham

21

braised fennel and tomatoes
finocchi e pomodori

2 small fennel bulbs
3 tablespoons butter
¼ cup water
2 tablespoons white wine

4 ripe tomatoes, peeled, quartered
Salt and pepper
Parsley, chopped

Cut off stalks of fennel; peel away stringy, pulpy outside layers of bulb. Cut in quarters; core. Slice into thin wedges.

Heat butter in heavy saucepan until melted. Add fennel, water, and wine. Cover; simmer approximately 10 minutes, until fennel is crisp-tender. Add tomatoes; season with salt and pepper; stir gently. Simmer 10 minutes.

Place in serving dish; garnish with chopped parsley. Makes 4 servings.

braised fennel and tomatoes

green noodles
fettuccine verde

1⅓ cups flour
½ teaspoon salt
4 egg yolks or 2 whole eggs
2 teaspoons olive oil
⅓ cup frozen chopped spinach, cooked, pressed dry in sieve

1 tablespoon oil
Melted butter
Freshly grated Parmesan cheese

Combine flour and salt in mixing bowl. Mix well. Make a well in center of flour mixture.

In blender jar combine eggs, olive oil, and spinach; blend until smooth. Add to dry ingredients; stir to form very stiff dough. Add small amount water, if necessary. Knead dough until smooth and elastic. Cover; let rest 30 minutes. Divide into 4 parts; roll out until paper-thin on floured surface. Cut into required shapes. Let dry on lightly floured surface 1 hour.

Cook in boiling salted water (float 1 tablespoon oil on surface of water) 5 to 7 minutes until al dente. Drain well.

Serve dressed with melted butter and fresh-grated Parmesan cheese or use according to recipe directions. Makes ¾ pound or 4 servings.

lasagna with meat and cream sauces

lasagna con carne e salsa alla crema

pasta
3 quarts water
2 teaspoons salt
1 tablespoon vegetable oil
8 ounces green or white lasagna noodles

meat sauce
4 tablespoons butter
2 tablespoons olive oil
1 medium onion, finely chopped
½ cup finely chopped carrot
½ cup finely chopped celery
¼ cup finely chopped parsley
1 pound meat-loaf mix (ground beef, pork, and veal)
¼ cup red wine
1 (16-ounce) can Italian style tomatoes, pureed
6 tablespoons tomato paste
½ cup water
1 teaspoon sugar
½ teaspoon salt
¼ teaspoon pepper
½ teaspoon crumbled sweet basil
½ teaspoon crumbled oregano

besciamella sauce
6 tablespoons butter
6 tablespoons flour
2½ cups milk
½ teaspoon salt
Pepper
¼ teaspoon freshly grated nutmeg
1 cup freshly grated Parmesan cheese for topping

Cook the pasta. Bring water and salt to boil in large kettle. Float oil on surface of water. Add noodles; cook according to package directions until al dente. Add cold water to pan to stop pasta from cooking further. Drain well; spread on paper towels.

Make meat sauce. Heat butter and oil in large saucepan. Add onion, carrot, celery, and parsley; sauté until tender. Add meat; sauté until lightly browned, breaking into small pieces with spoon while it cooks. Add remaining meat-sauce ingredients; mix well. Bring to boil; cover. Reduce heat to low; simmer 1 to 1½ hours or until thick.

Prepare Besciamella Sauce. Melt butter in heavy saucepan. Add flour; cook, stirring constantly, 2 minutes. Add milk all at once; cook, stirring constantly, until mixture thickens. Add salt, pepper, and nutmeg; stir well. Cool.

Lightly grease 13 × 9 × 2-inch casserole. Place thin layer of meat sauce in bottom of casserole. Top with ¼ noodles, spread with ¼ meat mixture, then with ¼ besciamella; sprinkle with ¼ cup Parmesan. Continue in this manner until all ingredients are used. Bake at 350°F 30 to 40 minutes, until heated through. Serves 6.

bean soup
zuppa di fagioli

2 cups dried white beans
8 cups water
1 teaspoon salt
6 tablespoons olive oil
1 large onion, chopped
½ cup diced bacon
2 cloves garlic, peeled, minced
1 stalk celery, chopped
1 carrot, peeled, chopped
4 tomatoes, peeled, coarsely chopped
1 teaspoon crumbled dried rosemary
1 teaspoon crumbled sweet basil
1½ cups cooked short pasta
Salt and pepper
Grated Parmesan cheese

Wash beans; pick over. Place in kettle with water; soak overnight.

Add 1 teaspoon salt to beans; simmer until soft. With slotted spoon, remove ½ beans; force through sieve or food mill. Add puree to remaining beans and liquid.

Heat oil in heavy skillet. Add onion, bacon, garlic, celery, and carrot; sauté until onion is golden. Add onion mixture, tomatoes, and seasonings to beans; cook 30 minutes. Add pasta; salt and pepper to taste. Cook 10 minutes.

Serve with grated Parmesan cheese. Makes 6 servings.

raw mushroom salad
insalata di funghi crudi

¼ cup olive oil
1 tablespoon lemon juice
1 clove garlic, peeled, minced
½ teaspoon salt
½ pound fresh mushrooms
3 scallions
3 small heads Bibb or Boston lettuce
1 tablespoon capers, drained

Combine olive oil, lemon juice, garlic, and salt; mix well.

Wipe mushrooms with damp cloth; trim; thinly slice.

Wash, trim, and thinly slice green tops of scallions. Combine mushrooms and scallions in small bowl. Pour dressing over mushrooms; marinate several hours.

Clean lettuce; crisp in refrigerator.

Place lettuce in large salad bowl. Add mushrooms and capers. Toss; serve immediately. Makes 6 servings.

artichoke omelet
frittata di carciofi

¼ **cup olive oil**
1½ **cups canned artichoke hearts, well drained**
1½ **tablespoons lemon juice**
6 **eggs**
½ **teaspoon salt**
Pepper
Parmesan cheese (optional)

Heat oil in large heavy skillet over moderate heat. Pat artichokes dry with paper towels; halve lengthwise. Sauté in hot oil until lightly browned. Sprinkle with lemon juice.

Beat eggs, salt, and pepper together well. Pour over artichoke hearts in skillet. Cook as you would omelet, lifting cooked egg with spatula and allowing uncooked egg to flow to bottom of pan. When top is almost set and bottom lightly browned, sprinkle with Parmesan cheese. Cook 2 minutes.

Cut into wedges; serve immediately. Makes 4 servings

stuffed breast of veal
petto di vitello farcito

stuffing
3 **tablespoons olive oil**
1 **medium onion, chopped**
½ **pound fresh spinach, stems removed, shredded**
¼ **pound ground veal**
¼ **pound ground pork**
1 **egg**
½ **cup fresh bread crumbs**
¼ **cup pine nuts**
⅛ **teaspoon nutmeg**
Salt and pepper

veal
1 **(4- to 5-pound) veal breast, boned**
Salt and pepper
2 **tablespoons olive oil**
2 **cups beef broth**
½ **cup white wine**
1 **carrot, peeled, sliced**
1 **stalk celery, chopped**
2 **bay leaves**
Salt and pepper
3 **tablespoons cornstarch**
3 **tablespoons water**

Make the stuffing. Heat oil in heavy skillet. Add onion; sauté until tender. Add spinach; sauté, stirring constantly, until wilted. Remove from heat; cool. Add remaining stuffing ingredients; mix well.

Have butcher cut pocket in veal breast for stuffing. Wipe meat with damp cloth; season with salt and pepper on outside and in pocket. Fill pocket with stuffing; skewer shut. Heat remaining oil in Dutch oven. Brown veal well on all sides. Add broth, wine, carrot, celery, and seasonings. Bring to boil. Cover; roast at 350°F 2½ hours, basting every ½ hour. Remove from oven. Take meat from pan; keep warm.

Combine cornstarch and water; mix well. Add to pan juices; cook over low heat until thickened. Remove skewer; carve veal breast. Serve with gravy. Makes 6 servings.

sweetmeat
panforte

This dessert resembles fruitcake.

1 cup shelled filberts	**½ cup sugar**
¾ cup blanched almonds	**½ cup honey**
½ cup sifted flour	**Confectioners' sugar**
1 cup mixed glacéd fruit	
1 tablespoon cinnamon	
2 tablespoons chopped mixed candied peels	

Toast filberts in moderate oven; rub in kitchen towel to remove skins.

Lightly toast almonds. Combine nuts, flour, glacéd fruit, cinnamon, and candied peels; set aside.

Combine sugar and honey in heavy saucepan. Bring to boil over moderate heat. Reduce heat to low; cook mixture undisturbed to soft-ball stage (238°F on candy thermometer). Pour into large bowl; add fruit and nut mixture; mix well. Place in 2 greased 7-inch-round cake pans (or substitute greased 10-inch pie plate). Bake at 325°F 35 minutes, until firm. Cool; dust with confectioners' sugar.

Serve cut in wedges. Makes 12 servings.

anise cookies
biscotti all'anice

These cookies are very crisp and are often used for dunking in coffee or in wine.

1 cup butter	**3 tablespoons anisette**
2 cups sugar	**5½ cups flour**
6 eggs	**1 tablespoon baking powder**
4 tablespoons aniseed	**2 cups chopped blanched almonds**
1 teaspoon vanilla	

Cream butter until soft. Slowly add sugar; mix well. Beat in eggs, 1 at a time. Add aniseed, vanilla, and anisette; mix well.

Sift flour and baking powder together; stir into egg mixture. Stir in almonds; chill dough 2 to 3 hours.

Lightly grease several cookie sheets. On lightly floured board form dough into flat loaves ½ inch thick, 2 inches wide, and as long as cookie sheets. Place several inches apart on cookie sheets. (You should have 6 loaves.) Bake at 375°F 20 minutes. Remove from oven; cool, Slice loaves diagonally into ½- to ¾-inch-thick slices. Lay slices, cut-side-down, close together on cookie sheet. Bake at 375°F 15 minutes, until lightly browned. Cool; store airtight. Makes approximately 100 cookies.

bow knots
cenci

1¼ cups flour	**½ teaspoon lemon rind**
1 tablespoon sugar	**2 tablespoons white wine**
Pinch of salt	**Vegetable oil for frying**
1 tablespoon butter	**Confectioners' sugar**
1 egg	

Combine flour; sugar, and salt in mixing bowl. Cut in butter. Make well in center of flour mixture. Add egg, lemon rind, and wine. Mix to form stiff dough, adding more wine if necessary. Turn out on lightly floured surface; knead until smooth and elastic. Cover; let rest 1 hour.

Roll dough ¹⁄₁₆th inch thick; cut into rectangles 3 × 4½ inches. Make 3 lengthwise cuts in each piece of dough. The strips formed can be intertwined to form knots.

Heat at least 1 inch cooking oil to 365°F; fry 2 at a time until puffed and golden. Drain on paper towels; sprinkle with confectioners sugar. Makes 15 pastries.

Venice (Veneto)

fish in sour sauce
pesce in saor

1 pound sole fillets, defrosted if frozen
⅓ cup flour
Salt and white pepper
6 tablespoons olive oil

sauce
2 tablespoons olive oil
1 medium onion, peeled, diced
1 carrot, peeled, diced
1 stalk celery, diced
½ cup white wine
½ cup white wine vinegar
1 bay leaf
1 teaspoon sugar
Salt
White pepper

1½ tablespoons pine nuts
1½ tablespoons dark raisins, soaked in warm water to plump

Wash fish; pat dry. Cut into serving-size pieces.

Combine flour, salt, and pepper on piece of waxed paper. Dredge fish in flour mixture.

Heat olive oil in heavy skillet. Over moderate heat brown fish few pieces at a time, without crowding. Drain on paper towels. Place in 9- × 9-inch glass baking dish.

In another skillet heat oil for sauce. Add onion, carrot, and celery. Cook, stirring constantly, until tender but not browned. Add wine, vinegar, and seasonings; mix well.

Pour sauce over fish. Sprinkle with pine nuts and raisins. Cover tightly; refrigerate at least 4 hours before serving.

Remove bay leaf; serve at room temperature with crisp bread as luncheon dish or antipasto. Makes 4 servings.

fish stew
brodetto di pesce

5 tablespoons olive oil
1 clove garlic, minced
1 pound (4 medium) potatoes, peeled, diced
1 pound firm-fleshed whitefish (flounder, cod, or snapper), cut into
  chunks
4 cups fish stock
1 (16-ounce) can Italian-style tomatoes, pureed or sieved
½ cup white wine
½ teaspoon crushed fennel seed
1 bay leaf
1 teaspoon salt
⅛ teaspoon crushed red pepper
Freshly ground black pepper
3 tablespoons chopped parsley

Heat oil in Dutch oven. Add garlic; sauté until well-browned;
discard. Add potatoes; cook, stirring constantly, until lightly
browned. Add fish, stock, tomatoes, wine, and seasonings. Bring to
boil; reduce heat to low. Simmer 20 to 25 minutes, until fish and
potatoes are tender.

Ladle into soup bowls; sprinkle with parsley. Serve with garlic
toast. Makes 4 servings.

fish stew

venetian minestrone

venetian minestrone
minestra alla veneziana

1½ pounds, lean round steak
3 tablespoons olive oil
1 large onion, peeled, sliced
1 clove garlic, minced
6 cups beef stock or broth
4 tomatoes, peeled, chopped
1 teaspoon crumbled dried oregano
½ teaspoon crumbled dried thyme
1 teaspoon salt
½ teaspoon pepper
½ cup long-grain white rice
½ pound savoy cabbage, shredded
3 tablespoons chopped fresh parsley
Grated Parmesan cheese

Thinly slice round steak across grain.

Heat olive oil in Dutch oven. Add onion and garlic; sauté until tender. Remove with slotted spoon; reserve.

Add round steak; brown well. Add beef broth, tomatoes, seasonings, onion, and garlic; bring to boil. Reduce heat to low; cover. Cook 1 hour, until meat is very tender. Add rice; simmer 20 minutes. Add cabbage; simmer 15 minutes.

Add parsley; ladle into soup bowls. Sprinkle with Parmesan. Makes 4 to 5 servings.

mixed seafood salad
insalata di frutti di mare

2 dozen mussels
2 dozen small clams
3 tablespoons olive oil

2 pounds small squid
½ cup white wine
1¼ pounds medium shrimp

dressing
4 tablespoons olive oil
2 tablespoons lemon juice
1 teaspoon Dijon mustard

Salt
Freshly ground pepper

2 tablespoons finely chopped parsley
Lettùce
Lemon wedges

Scrub mussels and clams well under cold running water.

Heat 3 tablespoons oil in large skillet with tight-fitting lid. Add mussels and clams; cover. Cook over medium-high heat, shaking pan occasionally, until shellfish open (approximately 10 minutes). Remove clams and mussels from shells; cool. Reserve juices; strain through sieve.

Wash squid; remove tentacles. Remove head, chitinous pen, and viscera; wash mantle well.

In large saucepan combine reserved juices from shellfish and white wine. Bring to boil over moderate heat. Add squid body and tentacles; cover. Simmer 10 minutes. Add shrimp; cook 15 minutes. (Squid should be tender and shrimp cooked through and pink.) Drain well. Shell shrimp; slice squid body into thin rings.

In large bowl combine clams, mussels, squid, and shrimp.

For dressing, combine oil, lemon juice, mustard, salt, and pepper.

Pour dressing over seafood; mix well. Sprinkle with parsley; marinate in refrigerator 2 hours.

Serve on beds of lettuce, garnished with lemon wedges. Makes 4 servings.

liver venetian-style
fegato alla veneziana

2 cups thinly sliced onions
2 tablespoons olive oil
2 tablespoons butter
½ teaspoon crumbled leaf sage
1 bay leaf
2 tablespoons dry white wine
1 pound calves' liver, sliced ½ inch thick
½ cup all-purpose flour
Salt and pepper
¼ cup cooking oil
1 tablespoon chopped fresh parsley

Sauté onions in olive oil and butter in heavy skillet until soft and lightly browned. Add sage, bay leaf, and wine. Cover; reduce heat to low. Simmer while cooking liver.

Cut liver into ¾-inch-wide strips 3 to 4 inches long; drain well.

Combine flour, salt, and pepper on plate.

Heat cooking oil in heavy skillet over moderate heat. Dredge liver in flour mixture; shake off excess. Fry part of liver until lightly browned. Drain; keep warm while cooking remaining liver.

Place liver in serving dish; top with onion mixture (remove bay leaf). Sprinkle with parsley. Serve with risotto on polenta. Makes 4 servings.

salt cod venetian-style
baccalá

1½ pounds salt cod
¾ cup olive oil
2 medium onions, peeled, sliced
1 clove garlic, peeled, minced
Flour
1½ cups milk
Fresh-ground pepper
2 tablespoons chopped parsley
2 tablespoons grated Parmesan cheese

Place cod in cold water to cover; soak 24 hours, changing water several times. Drain well. Skin and bone cod. Cut into serving-size pieces.

Heat oil in heavy skillet. Add onions and garlic; sauté until tender.

Lightly dredge cod in flour. Tightly pack into shallow casserole dish. Pour onion mixture over cod. Add milk to casserole; sprinkle with fresh ground pepper, parsley and cheese. Cover tightly with foil; bake at 250°F 4½ hours, stirring occasionally.

Serve with polenta. Makes 4 to 5 servings.

manicotti venetian-style
manicotti alla veneziana

1 (8-ounce) package manicotti noodles
Boiling salted water
1 tablespoon cooking oil

meat filling
1 pound meat-loaf mixture (ground pork, beef, and veal)
1 large onion, peeled, diced
1 clove garlic, peeled, minced
1 egg, well beaten
1 cup fresh bread crumbs
¼ cup finely chopped parsley
1 teaspoon crumbled sweet basil
Salt and pepper

sauce
6 tablespoons butter	1½ cups chicken broth
6 tablespoons flour	1 cup light cream
½ teaspoon salt	¾ cup freshly grated Parmesan cheese
White pepper	Nutmeg
¼ teaspoon ground nutmeg	Chopped parsley

Cook manicotti shells in large pan boiling salted water, with oil floating on surface, 15 minutes, until al dente. Drain well; rinse with cold water. Set aside.

For filling, in heavy skillet cook meat-loaf mixture, onion, and garlic over low heat until meat looses all red color. Break meat into small chunks as it cooks. Drain well. Combine meat mixture, egg, bread crumbs, parsley, and seasonings; mix well.

Stuff manicotti shells with filling. Place in lightly greased baking dish.

Make sauce in large saucepan. Melt butter; add flour; cook, stirring constantly, until bubbly. Add seasonings; stir well. Add broth and cream all at one time. Cook, stirring constantly, until thickened. Remove from heat; stir in cheese.

Pour sauce evenly over stuffed manicotti noodles. Sprinkle lightly with nutmeg and chopped parsley. Bake at 350°F 30 minutes. Serve immediately. Makes 6 to 8 servings.

mixed-meat brochettes
osei scampai

½ cup white wine
¼ cup olive oil
1 clove garlic, crushed
½ teaspoon crumbled sage leaves
2 pounds raw turkey-breast meat, cut into 1½-inch cubes
1 pound Italian sweet sausage links
24 mushroom caps
2 green peppers, cleaned, cut into chunks

In glass bowl or casserole combine wine, oil, garlic, and sage; mix well. Add turkey; stir to combine. Cover; let marinate 1 hour.

Prick sausages; simmer, in water to cover, 15 minutes. Drain; cool. Cut each sausage into 1½-inch pieces.

Grease 6 skewers. Alternately thread meats and vegetables on skewers. (Reserve turkey marinade for basting.) Grill or broil brochette about 8 inches from heat 20 minutes, until meats are cooked through. Baste occasionally, brushing with marinade.

Serve at once with rice, noodles, or polenta. Makes 6 servings.

chicken croquettes
croche di pollo

4 tablespoons butter or margarine
4 tablespoons flour
¼ teaspoon salt
⅛ teaspoon pepper
1 cup milk
2 cups finely chopped cooked chicken
½ cup finely minced ham
3 tablespoons freshly grated Parmesan cheese
2 teaspoons dried parsley flakes
¼ teaspoon poultry seasoning
½ cup flour
1 egg
1 tablespoon water
¾ cup fine dry bread crumbs
Oil for deep frying

Melt butter in heavy saucepan. Add 4 tablespoons flour, salt, and pepper; cook, stirring constantly, until bubbly. Add milk all at one time; cook, stirring constantly, until thick. Remove from heat. Add chicken, ham, Parmesan, parsley, nutmeg, and poultry seasoning; stir well. Chill 2 hours.

Form into round croquettes 1½ inches in diameter. Lightly coat with ½ cup flour.

Beat egg and water together in shallow bowl or pie plate.

Place bread crumbs on sheet of waxed paper. Dip croquettes in egg; roll in crumbs. Chill 1 hour.

Heat several inches oil to 375°F in deep-fat fryer. Fry croquettes a few at at time until golden. Drain on paper towels; serve immediately. Makes 4 servings.

stuffed chicken
pollo imbottito

1 (6-pound) capon or roasting chicken
½ pound hot or sweet Italian sausage (either bulk or links with casing removed)
2 tablespoons olive oil
½ cup finely chopped onion
1 clove garlic, peeled, chopped
1 cup raw long-grain rice
2 cups boiling water
1 cup cleaned sliced fresh mushrooms (or substitute a 4-ounce can drained mushrooms)
1 teaspoon chicken-broth granules
¼ teaspoon crumbled dried sweet basil
Salt and pepper
Olive oil for rubbing
6 medium potatoes, peeled

Wash chicken; pat dry.

In small skillet sauté sausage in oil until lightly browned. Add onion and garlic; sauté until lightly browned. Add rice; cook, stirring, until opaque. Add water, mushrooms, broth granules, and seasonings; cover tightly. Reduce heat to low; cook 15 to 20 minutes, until tender. Cool.

Stuff chicken with mixture. Truss body cavity shut. Stuff neck cavity; skewer shut. Pin wings close to body; tie legs together. Rub liberally with oil, salt, and pepper.

Grease roasting pan; place chicken in pan. Roast at 350°F (25 minutes to the pound). One hour before chicken is done, add potatoes to roasting pan. Baste occasionally with pan juices. Makes 6 servings.

shrimp broiled with garlic
scampi ai ferri

2 pounds large or jumbo shrimp, raw, in shells
¾ cup olive oil
2 cloves garlic, crushed
1 teaspoon salt
½ teaspoon freshly ground pepper
¼ cup chopped parsley
Lemon wedges

Wash shrimp well. Slit down back almost to tail with very sharp knife. Devein shrimp; leave shell intact. Place in single layer in shallow pan.

Combine oil, garlic, salt, and pepper; pour over shrimp. Cover; refrigerate 2 hours.

Thread 4 to 5 shrimp (depending on size) on each skewer. Grill over hot charcoal fire or in broiler (4 inches from heat source) 4 to 5 minutes on each side. Baste with oil in which shrimp were marinated.

Serve immediately; sprinkled with parsley, topped with lemon wedges. Makes 6 servings.

green sauce
salsa verde

1 (1½-inch) cube Italian bread
1½ tablespoons white wine vinegar
2 anchovy fillets
1½ tablespoons olive oil
2 hard-boiled egg yolks
½ cup finely minced parsley
¼ cup chopped scallions
Salt and pepper

Soak bread cube in vinegar in small bowl.

Mash anchovy fillets with olive oil. Add to bread; mash together thoroughly. Mash in egg yolks. Add parsley and scallions; stir to combine. Season with salt and pepper. Makes ⅔ cup.

cornmeal pudding
polenta

¾ cup coarse yellow cornmeal
3 cups cold water
1 teaspoon salt

Combine cornmeal with ¾ cup cold water, stirring well.

In medium saucepan combine 2¼ cups water and salt; bring to boil. Slowly stir cornmeal mixture into boiling water. Cook, stirring occasionally, until very thick, approximately 40 to 50 minutes. Mixture should pull away from sides of pan.

Wet clean wooden cutting board; pour polenta onto center of board. Allow to set.

Serve warm with butter, or cool and fry to serve with meat sauce. Makes 4 servings.

rice with squid
risotto con seppie

2 pounds squid
¼ cup olive oil
1 medium onion, peeled, chopped
2 cloves garlic, peeled, minced
½ cup white wine
Salt and pepper
1 cup raw long-grain rice
1½ cups fish stock or chicken broth
Several strands saffron
1 teaspoon hot water
2 teaspoons chopped parsley
2 tablespoons butter

Thaw squid if frozen. Remove tentacles by cutting from head; reserve. Remove and discard head, chitinous pen, and viscera. Wash thoroughly; drain. Cut mantle into thin rings.

Heat oil in large skillet. Add onion and garlic; sauté until tender. Add squid rings, tentacles, and wine. Season with salt and pepper. Cover; simmer 20 minutes. Add rice and stock; mix well. Bring mixture to boil over moderate heat. Cover; reduce heat to low. Cook 20 minutes.

Dissolve saffron in hot water; stir into fish and rice. Add parsley and butter, cut into small chunks. Season with salt and pepper to taste; serve. Makes 4 servings.

sautéed sweet peppers
peperonata

3 tablespoons olive oil
1 clove garlic, peeled
2 large green peppers, cleaned, cut into strips
2 large red peppers, cleaned, cut into strips
1 pound tomatoes, peeled, cut into chunks
Salt and pepper
Chopped parsley

Heat oil in heavy skillet. Add garlic; cook over moderate heat until browned; discard. Add peppers; sauté, stirring constantly, 5 minutes. Add tomatoes and salt and pepper to taste. Simmer, uncovered, until mixture is thick.

Serve hot or cold garnished with parsley. Makes 4 servings.

rice with peas

rice with peas
risi-bisi

3 tablespoons butter
1 small onion, finely chopped
⅓ cup diced prosciutto ham
1 cup raw long-grain rice
2 cups chicken broth
1 (10½-ounce) package frozen peas
Salt and pepper
Grated Parmesan cheese

Heat butter in heavy saucepan. Add onion; sauté until tender. Add ham; sauté 2 minutes. Add rice; stir to coat with butter. Add chicken broth; heat to boiling. Add peas, salt, and pepper; stir well. Cover tightly; simmer 20 minutes, until all liquid is absorbed. Fluff with fork.

Sprinkle with Parmesan; serve. Makes 4 to 5 servings.

almond macaroons

almond macaroons
amaretti

1 (8-ounce) package almond paste
4 egg whites
¾ cup sugerfine granulated sugar
2 tablespoons cake flour
¼ teaspoon salt

Cut almond paste into small pieces. Work 2 egg whites into almond paste. Slowly add sugar, flour, and salt. Mix well after each addition. Work in remaining egg whites; mix until free of lumps.

Grease and flour cookie sheets. Drop almond paste mixture by 1-inch balls 2 inches apart on cookie sheets. Bake at 300°F 20 to 30 minutes, until lightly browned. Remove from cookie sheet while still warm; cool completely. Makes about 2½ dozen cookies.

Note: Cookies can be decorated with halves of blanched almonds or pieces of candied cherry before baking.

wine custard
zabaione

6 medium egg yolks
3 tablespoons sugar
1 pinch salt
¼ teaspoon vanilla extract
½ cup Marsala wine

In top of double boiler beat all ingredients together until foamy. Place top of double boiler over simmering (not boiling) water. Beat constantly with wire whip or eggbeater until mixture becomes thick and hot.

Pour into sherbert glass; serve immediately. Makes 4 servings.

Variation
Omit vanilla; add juice and grated rind of 1 lemon.

Rome (Latium)

asparagus with mayonnaise sauce
asparagi con salsa maionese

1 (10-ounce) package frozen asparagus spears, partially thawed
1 tablespoon melted butter
1 tablespoon dry sherry
2 teaspoons finely minced onion
¼ teaspoon salt
Dash pepper

mayonnaise sauce
1 egg
1 teaspoon dry mustard
1 teaspoon salt
Dash of cayenne pepper
1 cup olive oil
3 tablespoons lemon juice
Parsley
Paprika

Place asparagus in small casserole, separating spears.

Mix butter, sherry, and seasonings. Pour over asparagus; cover. Bake at 350°F 25 minutes, until crisp-tender. Cool; refrigerate.

In blender container combine egg, seasonings, and ¼ cup oil. Cover; blend thoroughly. Remove center portion of blender cover. With blender running, add ½ cup oil in small steady stream. Slowly add lemon juice. Add remaining ¼ cup oil in thin steady stream. Blend until thick and smooth. Scrape mayonnaise down from sides of blender occasionally.

Arrange asparagus on beds of Bibb lettuce; coat with mayonnaise. Garnish with parsley and paprika. Serve as first course. Makes 4 servings.

roman-style vegetable soup

roman-style vegetable soup

minestrone alla romana

½ cup finely chopped salt pork
1 large onion, peeled, diced
1 clove garlic
3 carrots, peeled, diced
2 stalks celery, sliced
1 parsnip, peeled, diced
½ bunch parsley, chopped
2 large chopped tomatoes
1 quart beef broth
1 (16-ounce) can red kidney beans, drained
1 teaspoon crumbled sweet basil
Salt and pepper
1½ cups uncooked wide egg noodles
Grated Parmesan cheese

Render salt pork in large pan over moderate heat. Add onion and garlic; cook until tender. Add carrots, celery, parsnip, parsley, and tomatoes. Stir well; add beef broth, kidney beans, basil, salt, and pepper. Bring to boil; reduce heat to low. Cover; cook 1 hour. Add noodles; simmer 15 minutes, until noodles are tender.

Serve sprinkled with Parmesan cheese. Makes 4 generous servings.

stuffed mushrooms
funghi ripieni

12 medium mushrooms
5 tablespoons olive oil
2 tablespoons finely minced onion
¼ cup finely minced prosciutto
⅓ cup Italian-style bread crumbs
¼ cup freshly grated Parmesan cheese
2 teaspoons chopped parsley
⅛ teaspoon garlic powder
Salt and pepper
Chopped parsley
Grated Parmesan

Wash mushrooms. Remove stems; reserve for another use. Hollow out mushroom caps with teaspoon; drain well; pat dry.

Place 2 tablespoons oil in bottom of small casserole. Dip outside of each mushroom cap in oil, swirling to coat.

In small skillet heat 3 tablespoons oil. Add onion; sauté until tender. Remove from heat. Add prosciutto, bread crumbs, cheese, and seasonings; mix well. Fill mushrooms with bread-crumb mixture. Bake uncovered at 350°F 30 minutes. Makes 2 to 4 servings, depending on how many other antipasto dishes are served.

pickled green-bean salad
insalata di fagiolini

1 (16-ounce) can green beans, drained
2 tablespoons chopped onion
2 tablespoons chopped celery
2 tablespoons chopped green pepper
¼ cup olive oil
2 tablespoons wine vinegar
½ teaspoon crumbled sweet basil
Salt and pepper

In mixing bowl combine green beans, onion, celery, and green pepper.

Mix oil, vinegar, and seasonings; pour over vegetables. Mix gently. Refrigerate at least 4 hours before serving.

Serve on beds of lettuce or in lettuce cups. Makes 4 servings.

beef braised with cloves
manzo alla romana

1 (4-pound) beef rump or bottom-round roast
12 cloves
Salt and freshly ground pepper
3 tablespoons olive oil
½ cup chopped onion
¼ cup chopped celery
¼ cup chopped carrot
1 clove garlic, peeled, chopped
½ cup dry red wine
2 cups beef broth
½ cup tomato sauce
1 teaspoon crumbled oregano
1 bay leaf
4 slices bacon

Wipe roast with damp cloth. Stud with cloves; rub with salt and pepper.

Heat oil in Dutch oven. Brown meat well on all sides. Remove from pan and drain off excess fat. Add to the juice onion, celery, carrot, and garlic; sauté until tender. Add wine, broth, tomato sauce, oregano, and bay leaf. Bring to boil. Reduce heat to low; place roast in pan. Place bacon on roast. Cover; simmer 3 hours.

Slice meat; serve with pan juices, accompanied by plain pasta or potatoes. Makes 8 servings.

chicken hunter's-style
pollo alla cacciatora

1 (2½-pound) frying chicken, cut up
½ cup flour
Salt and pepper
⅓ cup olive oil
1 medium onion, peeled, sliced
1 green pepper, cleaned, sliced lengthwise
1 clove garlic, minced
1 (16-ounce) can plum tomatoes
¼ cup dry white wine
½ pound mushrooms, cleaned, sliced

Wash chicken well; pat dry.

Combine flour, salt, and pepper; dredge chicken well.

Heat oil in large skillet. Add chicken; brown well on all sides. Remove from pan. Add onion, green pepper, and garlic; sauté until tender. Drain off fat remaining in pan.

Break tomatoes into pieces with fork; add to skillet. Add wine; stir well. Bring mixture to boil over moderate heat. Add chicken; cover. Reduce heat; simmer 45 minutes. Add mushrooms; cook 15 to 20 minutes, until chicken and mushrooms are tender. Makes 4 servings.

turkey-breast cutlets with lemon and wine sauce
petti di tacchino piccata

2 tablespoons flour
3 tablespoons freshly grated Parmesan cheese
½ teaspoon salt
¼ teaspoon white pepper
¼ teaspoon nutmeg
1 egg, well beaten
½ cup milk
1 pound raw boneless turkey breast
Flour
4 tablespoons sweet butter
⅓ cup dry white wine
Juice of ½ lemon
Chopped fresh parsley for garnish
Lemon wedges

In shallow bowl combine flour, cheese, salt, pepper, and nutmeg. Add egg and milk; beat until well blended.

Skin turkey breast; cut crosswise into 6 slices. Pound with meat mallet or side of plate until thin. Dredge lightly in flour; shake off excess.

Heat butter in large heavy skillet over moderate heat until foam subsides. Dip turkey in batter; fry until golden. Remove from pan; keep warm. When all turkey is cooked, add wine to skillet. Cook over low heat 2 minutes, stirring to loosen browned bits from pan. Add lemon juice; mix well.

Pour sauce over turkey cutlets; sprinkle with chopped parsley. Serve immediately with lemon wedges. Makes 4 servings.

fried salt cod
baccalá fritto

1 pound salt cod
1 cup all-purpose flour
1 teaspoon baking powder
1 egg, well beaten
¾ cup water
1 tablespoon olive oil
Flour for dredging

Soak cod in cold water to cover at least 12 hours. Change water several times. Drain fish well. Remove any skin and bones; dry well with paper towels.

Combine flour and baking powder in mixing bowl. Add egg, water, and oil; beat until smooth. Dredge fish lightly in flour; dip in batter, coating well. Fry in 1½ inches hot oil (375°F), turning once. Fish should be golden brown and crisp. Drain fish on paper towels; keep warm in oven until all fish is cooked.

Serve immediately with Green Sauce (see Index). Makes 4 servings.

pork with celery
maiale affogato

2 tablespoons olive oil
1 clove garlic, peeled
1½ pounds lean boneless pork cubes, approximately 1½ inches square
1 medium onion, finely chopped
½ cup dry red wine
1 cup beef broth
1 cup plum tomatoes, drained, chopped
1 carrot, peeled, minced
1 teaspoon crumbled marjoram
¾ teaspoon salt
½ teaspoon pepper
2½ cups sliced celery

Heat oil in large heavy saucepan. Add garlic; sauté until golden. Remove from pan; discard. Add pork; brown well on all sides. Push pork to side of pan. Add onion; sauté until tender. Add wine, broth, tomatoes, carrot, and seasonings; bring to boil. Reduce heat to low. Cover; cook 1½ hours. Add celery; cook 20 minutes. (Pork should be tender and celery crisp-tender.)

Serve with plain pasta or gnocchi. Makes 4 servings.

broth with beaten egg
stracciatella

Literally translated, "stracciatella" means torn to rags.

4 cups clear broth (homemade or canned)
2 eggs
2 tablespoons freshly grated Parmesan cheese
1 tablespoon minced parsley
Freshly grated Parmesan cheese

Bring broth to boil in medium saucepan.

Beat eggs, cheese, and parsley together. Add mixture to boiling broth, beating constantly with wire whisk. Cook, while beating, 1 minute.

Serve immediately, garnished with additional grated cheese. Makes 4 servings.

fettuccine with zucchini and mushrooms
fettuccine con zucchini e funghi

sauce
½ pound mushrooms
1¼ pounds young zucchini squash
¾ cup (1½ sticks) butter
1 cup heavy cream

fettuccine
1 pound fettuccine noodles
Boiling salted water
1 tablespoon olive oil
¾ cup freshly grated Parmesan cheese
½ cup chopped parsley (preferably Italian flat-leaf parsley)
Salt and white pepper
Freshly grated Parmesan cheese

Wipe mushrooms with damp cloth, or wash if much dirt is adhering to them; pat dry with paper towels. Trim as necessary; slice.

Scrub zucchini; slice into julienne strips.

Melt ¼ cup (½ stick) butter in large heavy skillet over moderate heat. Add mushrooms; sauté 4 minutes. Add zucchini; sauté 3 minutes. Add cream and remaining butter, cut into small pieces. Reduce heat to low. Heat through, stirring gently.

Meanwhile, cook noodles in large amount of boiling salted water with oil floating on surface. Consult package directions for cooking times but test frequently so noodles are al dente. Drain well. Place noodles in warm bowl. Add Parmesan and parsley; toss lightly. Add sauce, salt, and pepper; lightly toss with 2 forks.

Place on warm platter; serve with freshly grated Parmesan. Makes 4 main-dish servings or serves 6 as a pasta course.

stuffed artichokes roman-style
carciofi ripieni alla romana

4 large artichokes
1 lemon
¾ cup dry bread crumbs
¾ cup fresh-grated Romano or Parmesan cheese
2 cloves garlic, peeled, finely minced
3 tablespoons minced parsley
1 tablespoon crumbled dried mint
Salt and pepper
1½ sticks (12 tablespoons) butter, melted

Wash artichokes. Break off stems; discard. Discard discolored outer leaves. With sharp knife cut off top of artichoke 1 inch below tip. Snip off sharp tips of leaves. Trim artichoke base with knife so it sits flat and level. Rub cut surfaces with lemon.

In stainless steel or enamel pot bring 2½ inches water to rolling boil. Add juice of ½ lemon. Add artichokes. Cover; cook 15 minutes. Drain upside down in bowl. Pull out centers of artichokes; with small spoon scrape out the choke.

Combine bread crumbs, cheese, garlic, parsley, mint, salt, and pepper; mix well. Stuff mixture between leaves and into center of each artichoke.

Place artichokes upright in large saucepan, tightly packed in pan. Drizzle each with 3 tablespoons melted butter; be sure to get butter between leaves. Add ½ inch hot water to pan. Bring to boil over moderate heat. Cover; bake at 400°F 1 hour, until artichokes are tender. Makes 4 servings.

lamb roast roman-style
abbacchio alla romana

1 (3-pound) boned and rolled lamb roast (leg or shoulder)
2 cloves garlic, peeled, cut into slivers
1 teaspoon crumbled dried rosemary
½ teaspoon crumbled dried marjoram
Freshly ground pepper
3 slices bacon, cut in half

anchovy sauce
2 anchovy fillets
1½ tablespoons olive oil
1½ tablespoons lemon juice
1 tablespoon fresh bread crumbs
½ cup chopped parsley
1 teaspoon freshly grated lemon rind
½ teaspoon crumbled rosemary

Wipe meat with damp cloth. Cut slits in top; place garlic sliver in each slit. Rub roast with rosemary, marjoram, and pepper. Place in roast pan, fat-side-up. Place bacon slices, slightly overlapping, over top of roast. Roast at 325°F 2¼ hours (internal temperature of 170°F). Roast should still be pink when sliced.

While lamb cooks, prepare sauce. Mash anchovy fillets with oil. Stir in lemon juice and bread crumbs. Add remaining ingredients; stir well. Refrigerate until ready for use.

Serve lamb roast with sauce, steamed broccoli, and tomato salad. Potatoes can also be pan-roasted with lamb. Makes 4 to 5 servings.

lamb roast roman-style

stuffed pasta with tomato sauce
cannelloni

pasta
15 (4½ × 5-inch) paper-thin pieces fresh pasta dough or 15 entree crepes

sauce
1 large onion, peeled
2 cloves garlic, peeled, minced
2 ounces slab bacon
2 cups Italian-style plum tomatoes (undrained)
¼ pound mushrooms, sliced
3 tablespoons tomato paste
3 tablespoons red wine
Salt and pepper

filling
2 tablespoons olive oil
1 large onion, peeled, chopped
1 clove garlic, peeled, finely minced
1 pound lean ground beef
2 chicken livers
1 (10-ounce) package frozen chopped spinach, defrosted
2 eggs, beaten
½ cup freshly grated Parmesan cheese
½ teaspoon crumbled oregano
Salt and pepper

garnish
¼ cup grated Parmesan cheese
2 tablespoons melted butter

Cook pasta, if used, in large amount of boiling salted water 5 minutes, until just tender. Drain well; place on paper towels to dry.

While noodles cook, begin sauce. Finely mince onion, garlic, and bacon together. Transfer mixture to heavy skillet; sauté over moderate heat until mixture begins to brown. Add tomatoes; break up with fork. Add remaining sauce ingredients; stir well. Cover; simmer 20 minutes.

To make filling, heat oil in large skillet. Add onion and garlic; sauté until tender. Add ground beef; sauté, breaking up into small pieces, 5 minutes. Add livers; cook until meat is browned. Remove livers; finely chop. Drain meat mixture. Combine meat and livers in large mixing bowl.

Place spinach in sieve; press dry with back of spoon. Add to meat mixture along with remaining filling ingredients; mix well.

Place 3 tablespoons filling on each pasta rectangle or crepe; roll up jelly-roll fashion.

Pour thin layer of sauce in bottom of shallow casserole dish. Place pasta rolls close together in dish. Cover with remaining sauce. Garnish with cheese; drizzle with butter. Bake at 350°F 30 minutes. Makes 4 to 5 servings.

Cut pasta dough into 4½ × 5-inch rectangles.

Prepare filling.

Fill pasta; roll firmly and seal.

Boil cannelloni 5 minutes.

Prepare sauce.

Cover boiled cannelloni with sauce and parmesan cheese.

preparation of stuffed pasta with tomato sauce

italian trifle
zuppa inglese

pastry cream
1 cup milk
½ cup sugar
2 tablespoons cornstarch
Pinch of salt
3 egg yolks
1 teaspoon vanilla extract

cake
1 recipe Pan Di Spagna (see Index), baked, completely cooled
3 tablespoons rum
¼ cup apricot jam

meringue
5 egg whites
¼ teaspoon cream of tartar
1 cup powdered sugar

In medium saucepan heat milk to boiling point over moderate heat. Combine sugar, cornstarch, and salt; mix well. Stir into hot milk. Cook, stirring constantly, until thickened. Remove from heat.

In small bowl beat egg yolks well. Pour small amount of hot mixture into eggs; beat well. Slowly add remaining hot mixture, beating well. Return to heat. Cook, stirring constantly, until mixture bubbles. Stir in vanilla; cool completely.

Cut sponge cake into 3 equal layers. Place 1 layer on cookie sheet. Sprinkle with 1 tablespoon rum; spread with 2 tablespoons jam. Spread with ½ pastry cream. Top with another cake layer. Sprinkle with 1 tablespoon rum; spread with 2 tablespoons jam. Spread with remaining pastry cream. Top with last cake layer; sprinkle with remaining rum.

Combine egg whites and cream of tartar in large mixing bowl. Beat until foamy. Slowly add sugar, tablespoon at a time. Continue beating until stiff and glossy. Spread layer of meringue over top and sides of cake. Put remaining meringue in pastry bag; decorate cake.

Bake in preheated 350°F oven about 15 minutes, until golden. Cool.

Carefully transfer to serving dish. Chill. Makes 8 to 10 servings.

italian trifle

broccoli
roman-style
broccoli alla romana

1 pound fresh young broccoli
3 tablespoons olive oil
1 clove garlic
Salt and pepper

Cut off dry ends of broccoli stalks. Incise bottoms of stalks with 4 gashes. Parboil in boiling salted water until crisp-tender. Drain well.

Heat oil in large heavy saucepan. Add garlic; sauté until golden. Discard garlic. Add broccoli; sauté, stirring constantly, 5 minutes. Season with salt and pepper to taste.

Serve topped with oil from pan. Makes 4 servings.

eggplant
parmigiana
melanzana parmigiana

sauce
¼ cup olive oil
1 pound ground round steak (or lean ground beef)
1 medium onion, chopped
1 clove garlic, peeled, chopped
½ cup chopped celery
½ cup chopped green pepper
1 (15-ounce) can tomato sauce
1 (6-ounce) can tomato paste
1 (16-ounce) can Italian plum tomatoes, broken up with fork
¾ teaspoon crumbled mixed Italian seasoning

eggplant and filling
1 medium eggplant
1 egg
2 tablespoons water
Fine dry bread crumbs
½ cup cooking oil
1 cup ricotta cheese
1 (8-ounce) ball mozzarella cheese, thinly sliced
½ cup freshly grated Parmesan cheese

Heat oil in heavy skillet. Add ground round, onion, garlic, celery, and green pepper. Cook, stirring until lightly browned. Drain well. Add remaining sauce ingredients; mix well. Bring to boil over moderate heat. Reduce heat to low. Cover; simmer 1 hour.

Peel eggpplant; cut into ¼- to ½-inch slices. Soak in cold salted water 30 minutes. Drain well; pat dry with paper towels.

Beat egg and water together in shallow plate. Place bread crumbs on sheet of waxed paper. Dip eggplant in egg mixture, then bread crumbs, coating well.

Heat cooking oil in heavy skillet. Brown eggplant slices, few at a time, over moderate heat. Drain on paper towels.

In 13 × 9 × 2-inch casserole dish place layer of half of eggplant slices. Dot with half of ricotta; top with half of mozzarella. Spoon half of sauce mixture evenly over cheese. Repeat layers, ending with tomato sauce.

Sprinkle with Parmesan. Bake at 350°F 60 minutes. Makes 8 servings.

peas with ham
pisselli con prosciutto

2 tablespoons butter
1 small onion, minced
⅛ pound prosciutto, diced
1 (10½-ounce) package frozen peas
1 tablespoon water

Melt butter in heavy saucepan. Add onion; sauté until tender. Add remaining ingredients; stir well. Cover pan tightly; simmer over low heat approximately 10 minutes. Check to be sure peas are tender. Cooking time can vary, depending on age and size of peas. Makes 4 servings.

rice fritters
suppli

4 cups water
1 tablespoon instant chicken-broth granules
2 cups raw long-grain rice
2 whole eggs, well beaten
½ cup grated Parmesan cheese

filling
3 tablespoons olive oil
⅓ cup finely minced onion
¼ cup chopped celery
½ pound lean ground beef
⅓ cup tomato paste
⅓ cup water
1 teaspoon crumbled basil
⅓ cup cooked peas

or
1 pound ricotta cheese can be used in place of above filling

coating
2 eggs, well beaten
1 cup dry bread crumbs
Oil for frying

Combine water and broth granules in large saucepan. Bring to boil. Add rice; stir well. Cover; reduce heat to low. Cook 20 minutes, until all liquid is absorbed. Cool rice mixture. Stir in eggs and cheese. Refrigerate 1 hour.

Meanwhile, make filling. Heat oil in heavy skillet. Add onion and celery; sauté until tender. Remove from skillet with slotted spoon. Add ground beef; sauté until lightly browned. Drain well. Add tomato paste, water, basil, and sautéed vegetables. Bring to boil; reduce heat to low. Simmer until thick. Stir in peas. Cool.

To form fritters, place heaping tablespoon rice in palm of hand. Top with ¾ tablespoon filling and another ½ tablespoon rice. Form into ball. If using ricotta, follow same method.

Beat eggs well. Dip rice fritters in egg; roll in crumbs. Refrigerate at least 1 hour.

Heat 3 inches oil to 365°F in medium saucepan. Fry few at a time until golden.

Drain on paper towels; serve with tomato or marinara sauce if desired. Makes about 30 fritters or 6 servings.

coffee ice
granita di caffé

2 cups water
1 cup sugar
4 cups espresso coffee (fresh or made from instant according to
     package directions)
½ cup whipping cream
½ teaspoon vanilla
2 tablespoons sugar
Chopped pistachio nuts (optional)

Combine water and sugar in small heavy saucepan. Bring to boil over moderate heat, stirring until sugar is dissolved. Reduce heat to low. Cook, stirring occasionally, 3 to 4 minutes, until mixture is syrupy. Combine with espresso, mixing well; cool. Place in freezer trays in zero-degree freezer. Freeze 3 hours; stir several times the first hour, until firm ice is formed.

Whip cream, vanilla, and sugar until stiff.

Empty coffee ice into blender; whirl briefly to break up ice crystals. Place in chilled sherbert glasses; top with whipped cream.

Sprinkle with chopped pistachio nuts. Makes 6 servings.

sponge cake
pan di spagna

3 large eggs
1 cup granulated sugar
⅓ cup water
1 cup cake flour
1 teaspoon baking powder
¼ teaspoon salt
1 teaspoon grated lemon peel

Line 15 × 10½ × 1-inch baking pan with waxed paper. Grease paper well.

Preheat oven to 375°F.

Beat eggs in mixing bowl until thick and lemon-colored. Slowly add sugar to eggs; beat until mixture is pale in color and double in volume. Add water; blend on low speed.

Combine flour, baking powder, and salt. Gradually add flour mixture and lemon peel; beat until batter is smooth.

Spread evenly in prepared pan. Bake at 375°F 12 to 15 minutes, until pick inserted in cake comes out clean.

Turn out on tea towel; remove paper. Cool completely. Makes 1 (15 × 10½ × 1-inch) layer.

pears poached in red wine
pere ripiene con vino rosso

4 firm ripe pears with stems (about 2 pounds)
1 tablespoon lemon juice
1½ cups rosé wine
¾ cup sugar
1 cinnamon stick
4 cloves
3 strips lemon peel
Lemon slices

Skin, halve, and core pears, leaving stems intact. Place in water with lemon juice to prevent darkening.

Combine wine, sugar, cinnamon, cloves, and lemon peel in large skillet. Heat to boiling, stirring to dissolve sugar.

Drain pear halves; add to skillet. Poach over low heat 10 to 15 minutes, until fork-tender (not mushy).

Chill (in syrup); serve garnished with lemon slices. Makes 4 servings.

Naples (Campania)

fried cheese sticks
fritto di mozzarella

1 pound mozzarella cheese
2 tablespoons flour
2 eggs
2 tablespoons water
1 cup Italian-style bread crumbs

sauce
1 tablespoon olive oil
2 tablespoons finely minced onion
1 (8-ounce) can tomato sauce
½ teaspoon garlic powder
½ teaspoon crumbled oregano
Salt and pepper

Oil for deep frying

Cut cheese into ½-inch slices, then into fingers or wedges. Coat lightly with flour.

Beat eggs and water together in shallow bowl. Dip cheese in egg mixture, then in crumbs; coat well. Refrigerate at least 1 hour uncovered.

Meanwhile, prepare sauce. Heat oil in small saucepan. Add onion; sauté until tender. Add remaining sauce ingredients; stir well. Cover; simmer 30 minutes.

Heat 2 inches oil to 380°F. Fry breaded cheese fritters, few at a time, until pale golden. Drain well on paper towels.

Serve immediately accompanied by tomato sauce. Makes 6 appetizer servings.

clam soup
zuppa di vongole

2 dozen cherrystone clams in shells
3 tablespoons olive oil
2 cloves garlic, peeled, minced
4 cups peeled ripe tomatoes, coarsely chopped
¼ cup white wine
4 tablespoons chopped Italian flat-leaf parsley

Scrub clams well under cold running water. Soak 30 minutes in cold water to cover.

Heat oil in large saucepan. Add garlic; sauté 1 minute. Add tomatoes and wine; bring to boil. Reduce heat to low; simmer 15 minutes. Keep warm.

In large frying pan or Dutch oven with close-fitting lid, bring 1 cup water to boil. Drain clams well; place in pan. Cover; steam 5 to 10 minutes, until clams open. (Discard any clams that will not open.)

Place clams in shells in warm soup bowls. Strain clam broth through cheesecloth; add to tomato sauce. Mix well; pour over clams in bowls. Sprinkle with parsley; serve with garlic toast. Makes 4 servings.

green salad with vegetables
insalata verde e vegetali

2 heads Boston lettuce
2 hard-boiled eggs, peeled, sliced
2 tomatoes, peeled, sliced
1 medium onion, peeled, sliced, separated into rings
1 green pepper, cleaned, sliced
½ cup stuffed green olives, sliced

salad dressing
4 tablespoons olive oil
3 tablespoons white wine vinegar
2 tablespoons finely chopped parsley
1 garlic clove, peeled, minced
1 teaspoon crumbled oregano
½ teaspoon salt
Freshly ground pepper

Clean lettuce. Wash; drain well. Break into bite-size pieces; place in salad bowl. Top with hard-boiled eggs, tomatoes, onion, pepper, and olives. Chill until serving time.

Combine salad-dressing ingredients; mix well.

At serving time, pour dressing over salad; toss gently. Serve immediately. Makes 4 servings.

green salad with vegetables

cheese turnovers

cheese turnovers
panzarotti

dough
2½ cups all-purpose flour
1 teaspoon salt
1 package active dry yeast
1 cup warm water
2 tablespoons olive oil

filling
1 (8-ounce) ball mozzarella cheese, shredded
1 cup finely minced prosciutto
½ cup chopped stuffed green olives
Pepper

1 egg
1 tablespoon water

Combine flour and salt in mixing bowl.

Dissolve yeast in warm water. Add yeast mixture and oil to flour. Mix to form stiff dough. Turn out onto lightly floured surface; knead until smooth and elastic. Place in greased bowl. Rotate to grease surface of dough. Cover; let rise in warm place until double in bulk (1½ to 2 hours).

To prepare filling, combine cheese, ham, olives, and pepper to taste; mix well.

Punch dough down. Place on lightly floured surface; divide into 12 equal parts. Roll each part to 5-inch circle. Spoon about 2 heaping tablespoons filling on ½ of each round. Fold over; moisten edges lightly with water; seal. Place on lightly greased cookie sheets. Beat egg and water together; brush turnovers with mixture. Bake at 375°F 20 minutes, until golden. Makes 12 turnovers (6 servings).

Note: Panzarotti can also be deep-fried. Heat at least 1½ inches fat to 360°F. Do not brush turnovers with egg. Fry until golden; drain on paper towels.

meat sauce for spaghetti
ragú

¼ cup olive oil
1 medium onion, finely chopped
2 cloves garlic, peeled, minced
¾ pound lean ground beef
½ pound bulk Italian sausage (sweet or hot)
1 (28-ounce) can Italian-style plum tomatoes (sieved or
   blenderized)
1 (6-ounce) can tomato paste
1 (6-ounce) can water
½ cup dry red wine
1 teaspoon crumbled mixed Italian herbs
1 teaspoon sugar
⅛ teaspoon crushed red pepper
Salt and pepper

Heat oil in large heavy saucepan. Add onion and garlic; sauté until tender. Add beef and sausage. Cook, breaking into small chunks, until lightly browned. Drain well. Add remaining ingredients; mix well. Bring to boil, reduce heat to simmer. Cook partially covered 2 hours, until thick.

Serve over hot cooked spaghetti or macaroni. Makes 4 servings.

meat sauce for spaghetti

marinated bean salad with tuna
insalata di fagioli con tonno

2 (16-ounce) cans cannelli beans, drained
1 (7-ounce) can white solid-pack tuna, drained; broken into chunks
¼ cup finely chopped onion
¼ cup finely chopped celery
¼ cup olive oil
2 tablespoons wine vinegar
½ teaspoon crushed dried sweet basil
Salt and pepper

In large bowl combine beans, tuna, and vegetables; mix gently.

Combine olive oil, vinegar, and seasonings; mix well. Pour over salad; mix gently. Cover; refrigerate at least 4 hours.

Serve on bed of lettuce with sliced tomatoes, black olives, and sliced hard-boiled egg; or serve as part of mixed antipasto tray. Makes 6 servings.

steak with tomato sauce
bistecca alla pizzaiola

This recipe is excellent for disguising a less-tender steak.

sauce
2 tablespoons olive oil
1 small onion, peeled, minced
2 cloves garlic, peeled, minced
1 (16-ounce) can Italian-style tomatoes
1 teaspoon crumbled oregano
Salt and pepper

2 tablespoons olive oil
3 pounds T-bone, porterhouse, or sirloin steak, 1 inch thick

To prepare sauce, heat oil in small skillet. Add onion and garlic; sauté until tender. Break up tomatoes with fork to form small chunks. Add tomatoes, oregano, salt, and pepper to skillet; stir well. Cover; simmer 15 minutes, until sauce begins to thicken.

In large heavy skillet heat remaining oil until very hot. Add steak; brown quickly on both sides, turning several times. Pour tomato sauce over steak. Cover; cook over low heat approximately 10 minutes (until done to taste). Remove steak from skillet; carve.

Serve topped with tomato sauce. Makes 4 servings.

ham and eggplant sandwiches
prosciutto e melanzane fritte

1 large eggplant
4 slices cooked ham, ¼-inch thick
4 slices (4 inches in diameter) provolone or mozzarella cheese
Flour
1 egg
3 tablespoons water
1 cup Italian-style bread crumbs
3 tablespoons olive oil

Cut 8 slices, each ¼-inch thick, from center of eggplant. Try to get all slices nearly same size. Reserve remaining eggplant for another use. Pare eggplant slices; soak in cold salted water to cover 30 minutes. Drain well; pat dry on paper towels. Make 4 sandwiches by placing ham and cheese slices between eggplant slices.

Dredge eggplant sandwiches lightly in flour, shaking off excess.

Beat egg and water together in shallow pan.

Place bread crumbs on piece of waxed paper. Dip sandwiches first in egg, then in crumbs, coating well.

Heat oil in heavy skillet. Cook sandwiches over moderate heat until well-browned on both sides. Drain on paper towels.

Place on cookie sheet; bake at 350°F 15 minutes.

Serve with tomato sauce if desired. Makes 4 servings.

sausage and vegetable skillet
salsiccia e vegetali

4 tablespoons olive oil
1 large onion, finely chopped
2 cloves garlic, peeled, minced
1 pound hot Italian sausage, casing removed, cut into 1-inch chunks
4 medium potatoes, peeled, cut into 1-inch cubes
2 green peppers, cleaned, cut into 1-inch chunks
2 red peppers, cleaned, cut into 1-inch chunks
2 cups tomato sauce
1 bay leaf
¼ teaspoon crumbled oregano
Salt and pepper to taste

Heat oil in Dutch oven. Add onion and garlic; sauté until tender. Add remaining ingredients; mix well. Bring to boil; reduce heat to simmer; cover. Cook over low heat 1 hour, stirring occasionally, until sausage is cooked through and vegetables are tender. Makes 4 servings.

savory veal patties with shells
maruzzelle con vitello

8 ounces seashell macaroni
4 tablespoons butter or margarine
¼ cup olive oil
1 medium onion, peeled, chopped
1 clove garlic, peeled, minced
4 (3 ounces each) frozen breaded veal patties
½ cup finely chopped parsley

Cook shells in boiling salted water 9 to 12 minutes, until tender. Drain; keep warm.

Meanwhile, in large skillet heat butter and oil over moderate heat until foam subsides. Add onion and garlic; sauté 1 minute. Remove vegetables with slotted spoon; add to drained macaroni. Pour ½ remaining butter and oil over shells; stir well to combine. Keep warm.

Brown veal patties over moderate heat in remaining butter and oil.

Serve shells on platter topped with veal. Pour pan drippings over veal patties. Pass Parmesan cheese. Makes 4 servings.

chicken with sausage
pollo con salsiccia

2 pounds cut-up frying-chicken parts
3 tablespoons olive oil
4 sweet Italian sausage links (½ pound)
1 medium onion, peeled, sliced
1 large green pepper, cleaned, sliced
1 cup sliced fresh mushrooms
1 (16-ounce) can Italian-style plum tomatoes, broken up with fork
3 tablespoons tomato paste
½ cup red wine
1 teaspoon crumbled sweet basil
Pinch of sugar
Salt and pepper

Wash chicken parts; pat dry. Heat oil in heavy skillet. Fry chicken, few pieces at a time, until golden, turning frequently. Remove from skillet; drain well. Add sausages to skillet; prick with fork. Fry until well browned. Remove from pan. Discard all but 3 tablespoons drippings.

Add onion, pepper, and mushrooms; sauté until tender. Add tomatoes, tomato paste, wine, and seasonings; stir well. Bring to boil. Add chicken and sausage. Cover; reduce heat to low. Cook 35 to 40 minutes.

Serve with plain pasta. Makes 4 servings.

chicken shoemaker's-style
pollo alla calzolaio

1 2½- to 3-pound frying chicken
2 tablespoons olive oil
3 tablespoons butter
Salt and pepper
1 clove garlic, minced
2 tablespoons chopped green onions
1 cup sliced fresh mushrooms
½ teaspoon crumbled dried tarragon
½ cup chicken broth
½ cup dry white wine
¼ pound chicken livers
1 tablespoon chopped parsley

Cut up chicken, bones and all. Cut into quarters. Remove legs, thighs, and wings. Cut each quarter into 3 or 4 parts. Cut each wing or thigh in half. Wash chicken; pat dry.

Heat oil and 2 tablespoons butter in large skillet over moderate heat. Add chicken; sauté until browned. Season with salt and pepper. Remove from pan.

Sauté garlic, onions, and mushrooms until tender. Add tarragon, broth, wine, and browned chicken pieces. Bring to boil; reduce heat to low. Cover; cook 30 minutes.

Melt remaining butter in small skillet. Sauté livers 5 minutes, until almost cooked through. Add to chicken; simmer 5 minutes.

Garnish with parsley; serve. Makes 4 servings.

cod with olive and caper sauce
baccalá alla marinara

sauce
2 tablespoons olive oil
¼ cup chopped onion
1 clove garlic, minced
1½ cups tomato puree
½ teaspoon sugar
¼ cup chopped pitted black olives
1 tablespoon drained chopped capers
½ teaspoon crumbled oregano
Pepper

1½ pounds cod fillets, defrosted if frozen

Heat oil in saucepan. Add onion and garlic; sauté until tender. Add remaining sauce ingredients; simmer 15 minutes.

Rinse fish under cold running water; pat dry. Place in lightly greased shallow baking dish in single layer. Pour sauce over fish. Bake at 350°F 25 minutes, until fish flakes easily with fork. Makes 4 servings.

tuna sauce for spaghetti
ragú con tonno

6 tablespoons butter
6 tablespoons olive oil
2 (7-ounce) cans tuna packed in olive oil
⅓ cup chopped parsley
2 tablespoons chopped capers
2 tablespoons lemon juice
¼ cup chicken broth
Salt and pepper

Heat butter and oil over moderate heat in heavy skillet.

Meanwhile, drain tuna; finely chop.

When butter has melted, add tuna, parsley, and capers to skillet. Heat through, stirring occasionally. Stir in lemon juice, broth, salt, and pepper.

Cook 1 pound spaghetti or your favorite pasta al dente. Drain well.

Place in large heated bowl. Add sauce; toss gently. Serve immediately. Makes 4 servings.

romano beans in a mist
fagiolini misto

1 tablespoon olive oil
2 tablespoons chopped onion
¼ cup chopped green pepper
1 (10-ounce) package Romano beans
½ cup chicken broth
⅓ cup sliced black olives
1 teaspoon cornstarch
2 teaspoons water

Heat olive oil in large saucepan. Add onion and pepper; sauté until tender. Add beans and broth. Separate beans with fork. Bring to boil. Reduce heat to simmer; cover. Cook 10 minutes, until tender. Add olives; stir.

Combine cornstarch and water; stir into vegetable mixture. Simmer 3 minutes, until sauce thickens slightly. Serve immediately. Makes 4 servings.

stuffed eggplant
melanzane ripiene

Stuffed vegetables are a Neapolitan specialty, and this recipe makes a very showy vegetable dish.

2 firm medium eggplants
Boiling salted water
2 small green peppers
2 small fresh tomatoes
1 (12-ounce) can artichoke hearts
½ cup olive oil
2 cloves garlic, peeled, minced
1 small onion, peeled, chopped
3 cups thickly sliced fresh mushrooms
1½ teaspoons crumbled oregano
1 teaspoon crumbled sweet basil
1 teaspoon salt
1 cup freshly grated Parmesan cheese

Cut eggplants in half lengthwise. Cut ½ inch from edges all around halves. Scoop pulp from center to form shells. Be careful not to pierce eggplant skin. Dice pulp. Parboil eggplant shells in 1 inch boiling salted water until barely tender. Drain carefully; set aside.

Clean green peppers; cut into 1-inch chunks.

Peel tomatoes; cut into wedges.

Drain artichoke hearts; halve.

Heat oil in heavy skillet. Sauté garlic, onion, and mushrooms until mushroom liquid evaporates. Add eggplant pulp; sauté until lightly browned. Stir in seasonings. Gently stir in peppers, tomatoes, and artichoke hearts; heat through. Stir in ½ cup Parmesan cheese.

Place reserved eggplant shells cut-side-up in lightly greased baking dish. Mound vegetable mixture in shells. Sprinkle with remaining cheese. Bake at 350°F 20 minutes. Makes 4 servings.

stuffed zucchini
zucchini ripiene

8 medium zucchini (7 to 8 inches long)

filling
½ pound lean ground beef
½ pound sausage meat
2 tablespoons Parmesan cheese
2 tablespoons chopped parsley
⅛ teaspoon garlic powder
Salt and pepper

tomato sauce
3 tablespoons olive oil
1 medium onion, finely chopped
2 cloves garlic, minced
1 (12-ounce) can tomato sauce
1 teaspoon crumbled oregano
Salt and pepper

Cut ends from zucchini. Using apple corer, hollow out center of squash, removing all seeds. Leave ¾-inch-thick shell.

In mixing bowl combine filling ingredients; mix well. Stuff zucchini shells with mixture.

Prepare sauce. Heat oil in Dutch oven. Add onion and garlic; sauté until tender. Add remaining sauce ingredients; mix well. Bring to boil over moderate heat. Add stuffed zucchini shells to sauce. Cover; simmer 1 hour.

Serve zucchini topped with tomato sauce. Makes 4 servings.

stuffed jumbo shells
lumache ripiene

16 jumbo shells (6 ounces)

tomato sauce
2 tablespoons olive oil
½ cup finely chopped onion
1 clove garlic, peeled, minced
1 (16-ounce) can peeled Italian tomatoes, pureed
3 tablespoons toamto paste
½ teaspoon sugar
½ teaspoon mixed Italian seasoning
Salt and pepper

filling
1 (10½-ounce) package frozen spinach
1 (16-ounce) package ricotta
1 egg, slightly beaten
¼ teaspoon ground nutmeg
Salt and pepper

½ cup freshly grated Parmesan cheese

Cook shells, according to package directions, in large amount boiling salted water until al dente. Drain; rinse with cold water. Set aside.

Meanwhile, make sauce. Heat oil in medium saucepan. Add onion and garlic; sauté until tender. Add remaining sauce ingredients; mix well. Bring to boil. Reduce heat to low; simmer ½ hour.

Prepare filling. Place spinach in sieve; press dry. In mixing bowl combine ricotta, egg, spinach, and seasonings; mix well.

Stuff mixture into cooked shells. Place side by side in lightly greased 9 × 9-inch pan. Pour sauce over shells. Sprinkle with cheese. Bake in preheated 350°F oven 30 minutes.

Serve with garlic bread and green salad. Makes 4 servings.

pizza naples-style

pizza alla napoletana

pizza dough
1½ cups all-purpose flour
½ teaspoon salt
1 package active dry yeast
½ cup warm water (105 to 115°F)
1 tablespoon olive oil

tomato sauce
1 tablespoon olive oil
¼ cup finely chopped onion
1 clove garlic, minced
1 (16-ounce) can Italian-style plum tomatoes, broken up with fork
2 tablespoons tomato paste
½ teaspoon crumbled oregano
½ teaspoon sugar
½ teaspoon salt

topping
Olive oil

8 anchovy fillets, halved
½ cup canned mushrooms, drained
1 cup shredded mozzarella cheese
¼ cup grated Parmesan cheese

First make crust. Combine flour and salt in mixing bowl. Dissolve yeast in warm water; add oil; mix well. Add to flour mixture. Stir to form stiff dough. Turn out on lightly floured surface; knead until smooth and elastic. Place dough in greased bowl; rotate to grease surface. Cover with towel; place in warm place to rise until double in bulk (1 to 1½ hours).

Meanwhile, make sauce. Heat oil in medium saucepan. Add onion and garlic; sauté until tender. Add remaining ingredients; stir well. Simmer sauce until thick (approximately 50 minutes).

When dough has doubled in bulk, punch down. Place on floured surface; roll to 12-inch circle of even thickness. Place on 12-inch round pizza pan. Bake in 400°F oven 12 to 14 minutes.

Remove from oven. Brush crust with oil; top with sauce. Arrange anchovy fillets and mushrooms on top. Sprinkle with cheese. Return to oven; bake 10 minutes. Remove from pan; cut. Makes 1 (12-inch) pizza.

Note: It is easy to have pizza ready in your freezer. Simply double above recipe. Make 2 shells. Bake second shell first for 13 minutes; cool completely. Package and freeze shell. Freeze remaining sauce. When ready to eat, defrost pizza shell and sauce; continue as above.

neapolitan cream cake

cassatta alla napoletana

This cake is an easy dessert to make for company.

1 (8 × 4-inch) pound cake
3 tablespoons amaretto or brandy

chocolate cheese filling
1 pound ricotta cheese
3 tablespoons amaretto
  or brandy
¼ cup sugar

3 tablespoons chopped candied fruit
3 tablespoons chopped
  semisweet chocolate

whipped topping
1½ cups heavy cream
1 teaspoon vanilla extract

¼ cup confectioners' sugar

Additional candied fruit for garnish
Chocolate curls

With serrated knife, slice pound cake into 4 equal horizontal slices. Brush layers with 3 tablespoons liqueur; set aside.

In small mixing bowl, combine ricotta, 3 tablespoons liqueur, and sugar; beat until smooth. Fold in candied fruit and chocolate.

Place 1 cake layer on serving platter. Spread evenly with ⅓ cheese mixture. Top with another cake layer; continue layering until all ingredients are used. Press cake gently together. Cover; refrigerate 2 hours.

One hour before serving, chill small mixing bowl and beaters. Pour (cold) cream into chilled bowl. Add vanilla; whip until foamy. Slowly add sugar; continue beating until cream is stiff. Spread sides and top of cake lightly and evenly with whipped cream. Place remaining whipped cream in pastry bag fitted with star tip; decorate cake.

Garnish with candied fruit and chocolate curls. Makes 8 servings.

italian crisp wafer cookies

pizzelle

Although a special iron is required to make these cookies, they are delicious and addictive! Pizzelle plates are also available for many electric waffle irons.

½ cup margarine, room temperature
⅔ cup sugar
4 eggs, well beaten
1 teaspoon vanilla extract or anise extract
1½ cups flour
1 teaspoon baking powder
Pinch of salt
½ cup finely chopped nuts (optional)

Cream margarine well. Add sugar; beat until light and fluffy. Add eggs and flavoring; beat well.

Sift together flour, baking powder, and salt. Slowly add dry ingredients to creamed mixture; mix well after each addition. Fold in nuts. Batter should be soft and sticky.

Lightly grease pizzelle iron; follow manufacturer's directions for baking. Use approximately 1 rounded teaspoon batter for each pizzelle. Discard first one or two cookies; they absorb excess oil from iron.

These cookies keep very well in airtight container or can be frozen. Makes about 3 dozen cookies.

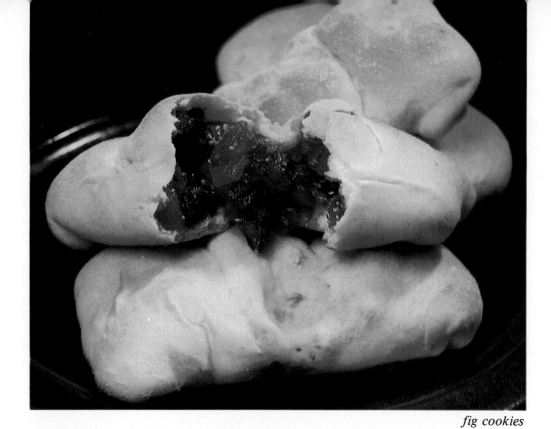

fig cookies

fig cookies
biscotti ripieni
con fichi

These cookies are traditional St. Joseph's Day treats!

fig filling
1 cup dried figs
½ cup light raisins
¼ cup candied cherries
¼ cup almonds
¼ cup hot water
2 tablespoons honey

dough
2½ cups flour
⅓ cup sugar
¼ teaspoon baking powder
½ teaspoon salt
½ cup butter
½ cup milk
1 egg, beaten

3 tablespoons butter or margarine
2 tablespoons sugar

First make filling. Put figs, raisins, cherries, and almonds through food grinder, or finely mince. Add water and honey; mix well. Set aside.

Make dough. In mixing bowl combine flour, sugar, baking powder, and salt. Cut in butter. Beat milk and egg together. Add to flour mixture; mix to form stiff dough. Turn out on lightly floured surface; knead 5 times. Roll to rectangle measuring 18 × 15 inches. Cut into 16 pieces.

Place 1 heaping tablespoon filling in center of each rectangle dough. Fold corners of each rectangle toward center. Place on lightly greased cookie sheet. Brush with melted butter; sprinkle with sugar. Bake at 350°F 20 to 25 minutes, until lightly browned. Makes 16 cookies.

INDEX

64